TO RECRUIT AND ADVANCE

WOMEN STUDENTS AND FACULTY
IN SCIENCE AND ENGINEERING

Committee on the Guide to Recruiting and Advancing
Women Scientists and Engineers in Academia

Committee on Women in Science and Engineering

Policy and Global Affairs

NATIONAL RESEARCH COUNCIL
OF THE NATIONAL ACADEMIES

THE NATIONAL ACADEMIES PRESS
Washington, D.C.
www.nap.edu

THE NATIONAL ACADEMIES PRESS 500 Fifth Street, N.W. Washington, DC 20001

NOTICE: The project that is the subject of this report was approved by the Governing Board of the National Research Council, whose members are drawn from the councils of the National Academy of Sciences, the National Academy of Engineering, and the Institute of Medicine. The members of the committee responsible for the report were chosen for their special competences and with regard for appropriate balance.

This project was supported by The Burroughs Wellcome Fund, Grant No. 1001461, 1001461.01, 1004684; The Howard Hughes Medical Institute, Grant No. 70200-50016; the Sloan Foundation, Grant No. B2000-17; the National Science Foundation, Grant No. HRD-0120774; and the National Academy of Sciences. Any opinions, findings, conclusions, or recommendations expressed in this publication are those of the author(s) and do not necessarily reflect the views of the organizations or agencies that provided support for the project.

Library of Congress Cataloging-in-Publication Data

To recruit and advance women students and faculty in U.S. science and engineering / Committee on the Guide to Recruiting and Advancing Women Scientists and Engineers in Academia, Committee on Women in Science and Engineering, Policy and Global Affairs, National Research Council of the National Academies.
    p. cm.
  Includes bibliographical references and index.
  ISBN 0-309-09521-2 (pbk.) — ISBN 0-309-54715-6 (pdf) 1. Women in science—United States. 2. Women scientists—United States. 3. Science—Vocational guidance—United States. 4. Science—Study and teaching (Higher)—United States. 5. Women in engineering—United States. 6. Women engineers—United States. 7. Engineering—Vocational guidance—United States. 8. Engineering—Study and teaching (Higher)—United States. I. National Research Council (U.S.). Committee on the Guide to Recruiting and Advancing Women Scientists and Engineers in Academia.
  Q130.T6 2006
  507.1'073—dc22

2006016786

Additional copies of this report are available from the National Academies Press, 500 Fifth Street, N.W., Lockbox 285, Washington, DC 20055; (800) 624-6242 or (202) 334-3313 (in the Washington metropolitan area); Internet, http://www.nap.edu.

THE NATIONAL ACADEMIES
Advisers to the Nation on Science, Engineering, and Medicine

The **National Academy of Sciences** is a private, nonprofit, self-perpetuating society of distinguished scholars engaged in scientific and engineering research, dedicated to the furtherance of science and technology and to their use for the general welfare. Upon the authority of the charter granted to it by the Congress in 1863, the Academy has a mandate that requires it to advise the federal government on scientific and technical matters. Dr. Ralph J. Cicerone is president of the National Academy of Sciences.

The **National Academy of Engineering** was established in 1964, under the charter of the National Academy of Sciences, as a parallel organization of outstanding engineers. It is autonomous in its administration and in the selection of its members, sharing with the National Academy of Sciences the responsibility for advising the federal government. The National Academy of Engineering also sponsors engineering programs aimed at meeting national needs, encourages education and research, and recognizes the superior achievements of engineers. Dr. Wm. A. Wulf is president of the National Academy of Engineering.

The **Institute of Medicine** was established in 1970 by the National Academy of Sciences to secure the services of eminent members of appropriate professions in the examination of policy matters pertaining to the health of the public. The Institute acts under the responsibility given to the National Academy of Sciences by its congressional charter to be an adviser to the federal government and, upon its own initiative, to identify issues of medical care, research, and education. Dr. Harvey V. Fineberg is president of the Institute of Medicine.

The **National Research Council** was organized by the National Academy of Sciences in 1916 to associate the broad community of science and technology with the Academy's purposes of furthering knowledge and advising the federal government. Functioning in accordance with general policies determined by the Academy, the Council has become the principal operating agency of both the National Academy of Sciences and the National Academy of Engineering in providing services to the government, the public, and the scientific and engineering communities. The Council is administered jointly by both Academies and the Institute of Medicine. Dr. Ralph J. Cicerone and Dr. Wm. A. Wulf are chair and vice chair, respectively, of the National Research Council.

www.national-academies.org

COMMITTEE ON WOMEN IN SCIENCE AND ENGINEERING

Lilian Wu, *Chair*, Director of University Relations, International
    Business Machines
Lotte Bailyn, T. Wilson Professor of Management, Sloan School of
    Management, Massachusetts Institute of Technology
Ilene Busch-Vishniac, Professor, Mechanical Engineering, The Johns
    Hopkins University
Ralph J. Cicerone, Former Chancellor, University of California, Irvine
    (until January 2005)
Allan Fisher, President and CEO, iCarnegie, Inc.
Sally Shaywitz, Co-director, Yale Center for the Study of Learning and
    Attention, Yale University School of Medicine
Julia Weertman, Professor Emerita, Department of Material Science and
    Engineering, Northwestern University

Staff

Jong-on Hahm, Director (until October 14, 2005)
Peter Henderson, Acting Director (from October 15, 2005)
Charlotte Kuh, Deputy Executive Director, Policy and Global Affairs
    Division
John Sislin, Program Officer
Elizabeth Briggs Huthnance, Senior Program Associate
Amaliya Jurta, Senior Program Assistant (through July 2002)

Preface

Although more women than men participate in higher education in the United States, the same is not true of careers in U.S. science and engineering (S&E). Women students and faculty in S&E experience higher attrition rates than men. Women students are awarded a large portion of S&E baccalaureate degrees, but at each subsequent stage the percentages drop. As a result, women faculty are scarce in S&E. As for women who do reach that level, studies have found that they are subject to gender disparities in salaries and workload (e.g., women have less time for research because more time is spent on counseling and service committees). Meanwhile, women advance more slowly through the academic hierarchy, and a higher proportion leaves academic employment.

Although their numbers are increasing, women also are underrepresented at the highest tiers of administrative positions. Many women have succeeded, as demonstrated by enrollments, degrees completed, and the presence of women faculty, deans, and university presidents. But their success also reveals the challenges that women face in trying to do so. This guide is about enhancing women's participation in academia in science and engineering.

In compiling this guide the Committee on Women in Science and Engineering of the National Academies sought to move beyond yet another catalog of challenges facing the advancement of women in academic S&E to provide a document describing actions actually taken by universities to improve the situation for women. In addition, the committee sought to show that the increase in participation of women can be achieved at research universities with stellar reputations—or to quote one university president, "Diversity versus quality is a false tradeoff." This guide, then, is a compendium of solutions that may be of use to other universities and colleges seeking to advance women in science and engineering.

This report has been reviewed in draft form by individuals chosen for their diverse perspectives and technical expertise, in accordance with procedures approved by the National Academies' Report Review Committee. The purpose of this independent review is to provide candid and critical comments that will assist the institution in making its published report as sound as possible and to ensure that the report meets institutional standards for objectivity, evidence, and responsiveness to the study charge. The review comments and draft manuscript remain confidential to protect the integrity of the process.

We wish to thank the following individuals for their review of this report: Robert Barnhill, University of Kansas; Joan Brennecke, University of Notre Dame; Susan Fiske, Princeton University; Linda Katehi, Purdue University; Maria Klawe, Princeton University; Melanie Leitner, Washington University; Laurie McNeil, University of North Carolina, Chapel Hill; JoAnn Silverstein, University of Colorado; Crispin Taylor, American Society of Plant Biologists; and Diane Renee Wagner, Stanford University.

Although the reviewers listed above have provided many constructive comments and suggestions, they were not asked to endorse the conclusions or recommendations, nor did they see the final draft of the report before its release. The review of this report was overseen by Mildred Dresselhaus, Massachusetts Institute of Technology. Appointed by the National Academies, she was responsible for making certain that an independent examination of this report was carried out in accordance with institutional procedures and that all review comments were carefully considered. Responsibility for the final content of this report rests entirely with the authoring committee and the institution.

Lilian Wu
Chair

A Note on Using This Guide

This guide addresses three issues—recruitment, retention, and advancement—for three populations of women: students, faculty, and administrators in science and engineering. The intended audience includes anyone interested in improving the position of women in these three areas. Most of the individuals with a stake in progress on this front are toiling inside university walls, but external groups, such as federal agencies or professional societies, will also find this discussion of interest.

Chapters 2-6 of the guide address in turn one of the issues combined with one population—for example, Chapter 2 explores the recruitment of students (although for administrators the three issues are combined into a single chapter). Each chapter is divided into three primary sections. A chapter begins with a brief discussion of the challenges facing women in the area (e.g., retention) addressed by the chapter. Much of this discussion is drawn from current literature. The rest of the chapter is then largely devoted to a description of the strategies pursued by the universities visited by the committee and others to meet these challenges. Each chapter concludes with a boxed summary that organizes the strategies by the faculty and administration levels most likely to implement them. Thus, for example, what can department chairs do to enhance the recruitment of female undergraduates? These substantive chapters are sandwiched by introductory Chapter 1, which briefly describes the challenges facing women students, faculty, and administrators and lays out the methodology used by the committee that produced this guide and the concluding Chapter 7, which summarizes the committee's findings and conclusions.

Special features throughout the guide are boxed summaries of the challenges and strategies as well as highlighted quotes from some of the students, faculty, and administrators (department chairs, deans, provosts, and presidents) who were interviewed during the committee's information-gathering site visits.

Contents

Summary   1

1   Introduction   5

2   Recruiting Women Students   14

3   Retaining Women Students   48

4   Recruiting Women Faculty   71

5   Advancing Women Faculty   86

6   Advancing Women to Executive Positions   100

7   Conclusion   109

References   118

Index   125

List of Tables, Figures, and Boxes

Tables

2-1 Percentage of High School Graduates Taking Selected
     Mathematics and Science Courses in High School, by Sex, 16
2-2 Percentage of AP Examinees Who Are Female, by Subject, 17
2-3 Percentage of Bachelor's Degrees Awarded to Women,
     by Field, 18
2-4 Freshmen Intending to Major in S&E, by Race/Ethnicity, Sex,
     and Field, 20
2-5 Freshmen Intending to Major in S&E, by Sex and Field, 24

4-1 S&E Doctoral Degrees Awarded to Women, by Field, 74
4-2 Male and Female Tenure-Track Faculty at Top 50 U.S. Educational
     Institutions, 76

5-1 Perception and Experience of Discrimination and Harassment by
     Gender, 89

Figures

2-1 Number of baccalaureate degrees awarded, by field and
     gender, 17
2-2 Female share of S&E graduate students, by field, 26

xiii

2-3   Number of women receiving bachelor's degrees, master's degrees, and doctoral degrees in science and engineering, 28
2-4   Percentage of women receiving bachelor's degrees, master's degrees, and doctoral degrees in science and engineering, 28
2-5   Postdocs in science and engineering, by gender, 29

4-1   Doctoral degrees received, by broad field and gender, 72

Boxes

2-1   Summary of Challenges, 30
2-2   Undergraduate Recruitment Strategies, 31
2-3   Graduate Student Recruitment Strategies, 39
2-4   Postdoctoral Recruitment Strategies, 44
2-5   Summary of Strategies for Recruiting Women Undergraduate, Graduate, and Postdoctoral Students, 47

3-1   Summary of Challenges, 55
3-2   Undergraduate Retention Strategies, 55
3-3   Graduate Student Retention Strategies, 65
3-4   Summary of Strategies for Retaining Women Undergraduate, Graduate, and Postdoctoral Students, 70

4-1   Summary of Challenges, 77
4-2   Strategies for Recruiting Women Faculty, 78
4-3   Summary of Strategies for Recruiting Women Faculty, 85

5-1   Summary of Challenges, 93
5-2   Strategies for Advancing Women Faculty, 94
5-3   Summary of Strategies for Advancing Women Faculty, 99

6-1   Summary of Challenges, 103
6-2   Strategies for Recruiting and Advancing Women to Executive Positions, 103
6-3   Summary of Strategies for Recruiting and Advancing Women to Executive Positions, 108

Summary

Although women have made great strides in becoming full members of the science and engineering (S&E) enterprise, they are still underrepresented among graduate students and postdoctorates and among faculty in science and engineering programs. The Committee on Women in Science and Engineering (CWSE) of the National Academies created the Committee on the Guide to Recruiting and Advancing Women Scientists and Engineers in Academia to produce a guide that would help those who have a stake in seeing more women in science and engineering accomplish that goal. Specifically, the committee was asked to prepare a guide that will identify and discuss best practices in recruitment, retention, and promotion for women scientists and engineers in academia.

> The issues that the guide will address are: (1) recruitment of undergraduates and graduate students; (2) ways of reducing attrition in science and engineering degree programs in the early undergraduate years; (3) improving retention rates of women at critical transition points—from undergraduate to graduate student, from graduate student to postdoc, postdoc to first faculty position; (4) recruitment of women for tenure-track positions; (5) increasing the tenure rate for women faculty; and (6) increasing the numbers of women in administrative positions.

The committee began by reviewing the literature on higher education programs and policies designed to recruit and retain women S&E students and faculty. The committee also decided to gather information by

1

visiting four universities recognized for successfully advancing and retaining women students, faculty, or leaders. During these site visits, committee members and staff interviewed students, faculty, and administrators to learn more about the latter's careers and experiences in academia. *To ensure that the interviewees would speak freely, the committee promised not to reveal their names or the names of the institutions visited.*

In its literature review and site visits, the committee sought to identify the strategies that some higher education institutions have employed to achieve gender inclusiveness in academic S&E and to use these four case studies as a way to gain a more detailed picture of women's participation in science and engineering (with a particular focus on research universities) with specific approaches that had worked at the visited institutions and could be adapted to others. The committee is able to present a variety of strategies that students, faculty, and administrators at higher education institutions, and outside interests, such as the professional societies, could use to better recruit, retain, and advance women in academic S&E.

The committee found that the term "successful strategy" might be used rather than "best practice." Although these institutions had made great strides, they still coped with issues present at all institutions of higher learning and throughout society overall. Additionally, a successful strategy at one institution may not have worked at another, thus "best" was not an appropriate moniker for these strategies.

One of the findings that resonated throughout the site visits and through the literature review is that women face multiple challenges—challenges that may lead to their attrition at key junctures in higher education. Some of the reasons for this attrition have to do with women's ambitions and career preferences; others stem from the demographic characteristics of female S&E students and faculty. Still others result from not enough being done by peers, departments, and institutions to create a climate that is as comfortable for women as it is for men. Fortunately, one of the main findings of the committee's study is that many policies are available to universities for facilitating the recruitment and retention of female students, faculty, and administrators. Some policies are better implemented by the top leadership—presidents, provosts, and deans—while others can be put in place by department chairs or individual faculty.

Policies to Enhance Student Recruitment

• Create and institutionalize a pervasive inclusiveness mandate on campus, with buy-in from the highest levels of the administration, and then dedicate resources to that mandate.

- Extend outreach to potential students at both the K-12 and undergraduate levels. Such outreach might take the form of summer science and engineering camps, lecture series, career days, collaborative research projects, and support for K-12 teachers.
- Examine the criteria used to select incoming students to ensure that unnecessary criteria are not filtering out women.

Policies to Enhance Student Retention

- Dedicate resources for female students, which could include an S&E dormitory or support for a women's S&E society on campus.
- Modify curricula and teaching to better engage the interests of female students.
- Create mentoring programs for students.

Policies to Enhance Faculty Recruitment

- Create and institutionalize a pervasive inclusiveness mandate on campus, with buy-in from the highest levels of the administration, and then dedicate resources to that mandate.
- Monitor the faculty hiring process to affirm the importance of women and confirm the presence of women in that process.

Policies to Advance Female Faculty

- Create mentoring programs for female faculty.
- Conduct periodic university studies of various issues affecting women, such as tenure process, salary equity, or climate.

Policies to Advance Women into Administrative Positions

- Create mentoring programs.
- Encourage faculty to network and to gain experience in administration.
- Promote peer encouragement of women who are or might be interested in pursuing administrative positions.

1

Introduction

Many studies have found evidence of gender disparities in U.S. academia and have raised serious concerns about the ability of U.S. universities to recruit and retain women faculty and students in science and engineering (S&E), now and in the future. Women students and faculty face challenges in academia.

Overall, one challenge facing most women is campus climate. At times, female students, faculty, and administrators may run into unfriendly, if not hostile, behavior from peers, colleagues, and superiors. Power relationships are magnified in the insulated and small setting of academia. Students are dependent on faculty (and access to faculty and their labs) to accomplish their research, for recommendations, and for entrée into the professional community. Faculty are dependent on peers during tenure and promotion cases.

In addition to an unfriendly climate, female students face challenges related to recruitment and retention. Much has been written about the difficulties encountered by universities in trying to encourage female secondary school students to enter university S&E programs. Likewise, concerns have been raised about the preparation that female students receive prior to postsecondary education. This guide will describe efforts by some universities both to increase the recruitment of female students by reaching down into secondary schools through various programs and to decrease the attrition of female students from S&E programs once they are enrolled.

Female faculty face a variety of different challenges. Percentage of women faculty members in science and engineering disciplines range from 10 to 30 percent (NSF, 2001). Women accounted for 10 percent of all faculty in physics in 2002, 14 percent of all faculty in astronomy in 2003, 18 percent of full-time faculty members at doctoral departments in mathematics in 2002, and 10 percent of tenured or tenure-track faculty members in engineering in 2003 (Gibbons, 2004; Ivie, 2004; Rankin, 2004). The underrepresentation of women is the most pronounced at the most prestigious research universities (NRC, 2001). Women science faculty are more likely to be employed by community colleges or institutions that do not offer a doctoral degree (Schneider, 2000).

Women faculty are less likely than male faculty to be full professors. As the National Science Foundation (NSF, 2004c) noted in its biennial publication *Women, Minorities, and Persons with Disabilities in Science and Engineering: 2004,* "Within 4-year colleges and universities, females are less likely than their male colleagues to be found in the highest faculty ranks. Women were less likely than men to be full professors and more likely than men to be assistant professors" (NSF, 2005). A survey of the top 50 university departments in several fields found smaller percentages of women at each successive rung of the professorial ladder from assistant to associate to full professor in every field but one (Nelson and Rogers, 2004).[1] In civil engineering in 2002, women accounted for 22.3 percent of assistant professors, 11.5 percent of associate professors, and 3.5 percent of full professors.

Women faculty receive lower salaries than their male counterparts.[2] According to a survey of the American Association of University Professors (AAUP), women's salaries for the academic year 2002-2003 remained behind men's salaries in every category (Fogg, 2003b).[3] Studies of salaries of science and engineering faculty find similar gaps (NRC, 2001; Ginther, 2001, 2004).

Another inequality is that women faculty spend more hours per week than men in the classroom, more time preparing for classes and advising students, and more time engaged in university service activities. "In sum, though all university faculty are expected to teach and to serve, as well as to research, male and female faculty exhibit significantly different patterns of research, teaching, and service. Men, as a group, devote a higher

---

[1]The exception was computer science; 10.8 percent of assistant professors, 14.4 percent of associate professors, and 8.3 percent of full professors were women.

[2]The current debate on gender inequality in salaries centers on how large the gap is and the reasons for it. See, for example, Ginther (2004).

[3]Perna's analysis suggests that women faculty are also less likely to receive supplemental earnings, such as from institutional sources or private consulting (Perna, 2002).

portion of their time to research activities, whereas women, as a group, devote a much higher percentage of their time to teaching and service activities than do men" (Park, 1996:54; also see Fogg, 2003a). There is some evidence that women are less satisfied in the academic workplace than men and are more likely to leave academia in the first seven years (Trower and Chait, 2002). Lower satisfaction may lead to unhappiness in the profession, leading to lower productivity, lower retention rates, and a reduced pool of future academics. Such unhappiness may be transmitted to the younger women just starting out and help to "scare a new generation away from academia" (Lawler, 1999). Finally, women faculty have higher attrition rates than men both before and after tenure (August and Waltman, 2004).

Although the percentages of female administrators are low, the good news is that today women are occupying a much larger percentage of presidencies at colleges and universities than previously. In 2001, 27 percent of presidencies at two-year institutions were held by women, compared with 8 percent in 1986. In doctorate-granting institutions, women held 12 percent of presidencies in 2001, three times the percentage in 1986 (Rivard, 2003). These institutions include the Massachusetts Institute of Technology, University of Pennsylvania, Princeton University, Brown University, and the University of California, San Diego. It is also more common to see female deans and provosts. Although some observers expect these percentages to rise, such an increase is not guaranteed; university policies can affect the likelihood that more women move into top administrative positions (Lively, 2000a).

The rest of this chapter describes common threads that run through both the literature review and the site visits. It then presents the research questions tackled by the study committee and the methodology used, and concludes with a brief description of the organization of this guide.

COMMON THREADS

Three common threads appeared to wind their way through the literature on women in science and engineering and the site visits made by the study committee. The first is that at each successive step, from undergraduate matriculation through a doctoral program and into an academic career, the number of women decline, thereby reinforcing a pattern of underrepresentation of women in academia. Nationally, in most fields of physical science the percentages of women dwindle as women move higher in standing. In the natural sciences, the percentage of women drops from 40 percent for undergraduates to 30 percent for Ph.D.'s to about 15 percent for professorial faculty. Similarly, the percentage of female tenured and tenure-track faculty in S&E fields declines from 34 percent for assistant professors to 27 percent for associate professors to about 13 percent for full professors.

A second common thread is that the "climate" of departments, and to a lesser extent of institutions, is chilly to women. A substantial portion of the literature—including universities' own self-assessments—bear out this point. Climate is a complex phenomenon that affects how members of a department, including students, get along with one another.

The third common thread is that the success of efforts to recruit and advance women in science and engineering depend largely on whether university leaders and administrators promote the institutionalization of change, not quick fixes, and on rapid implementation. It is easy to take ad hoc steps to try to deal with issues affecting a particular student, faculty member, or administrator. There may also be a temptation to "throw money at a problem" or set up a study committee. Such steps can produce improvements, but without support from the top levels of an institution, problems may persist.

> Promoting diversity takes leadership. It has to be an intentional effort; you can't just set the stage and back away.
>
> —University dean, during site visit

Those interviewed at the universities visited identified three challenges to making change endure. First, those at the highest university levels—president, provost, and deans—must be convinced to take change seriously and give it high priority and high visibility. Second, change must be institutionalized as opposed to a quick fix. An associate dean described an experiment in hiring more women by providing an open hiring fund. He found that all the money went quickly but produced few lasting results. Because the slots were viewed as "free," the departments did not make a strong effort to hire people who truly fit into their programs and had a good chance of success. Third, university bureaucracies must be convinced to move faster in implementing changes and hiring. Another dean, who came from industry, noted how difficult it is to act quickly at a university, "When I'm the president of a company and I find someone I want, I can hire her on the spot. Here the dean can say no, but he can't hire anybody. I have to convince the faculty that they want this person."

KEY RESEARCH QUESTIONS

In discussing the challenges faced by universities and academicians when trying to increase the percentages of women in science and engineering, members of the Committee on Women in Science and Engineering (CWSE) of the National Academies noted that some institutions seemed to attract significant percentages of women to their degree programs and as faculty. These institutions did not appear to be remarkably different from their peers on the surface—they were all research universities that had stellar reputations in academic circles. Two questions followed from this observation:

1. What are the more diverse institutions doing differently from their peers, which have seen smaller increases in the numbers and percentages of women?
2. What is involved in the creation of diversity-building initiatives?

From these two questions the concept for this project was developed.

THE COMMITTEE'S CHARGE

The Committee on Women in Science and Engineering of the National Academies sought to move beyond simply cataloguing the challenges facing the advancement of women in academic S&E. It wanted to provide a guide that would describe many of the policy responses actually implemented by universities in seeking to improve the situation for women—that is, policy responses that could be used as guidelines by other universities and colleges and applied as appropriate. The study committee was directed in its effort by the following charge from CWSE:

> This project will prepare a guide that will identify and discuss best practices in recruitment, retention, and promotion for women scientists and engineers in academia. The issues that the guide will address are: (1) recruitment of undergraduates and graduate students; (2) ways of reducing attrition in science and engineering degree programs in the early undergraduate years; (3) improving retention rates of women at critical transition points—from undergraduate to graduate student, from graduate student to postdoc, postdoc to first faculty position; (4) recruitment of women for tenure-track positions; (5) increasing the tenure rate for women faculty; and (6) increasing the numbers of women in administrative positions.

METHODOLOGY

To craft this guide, the study committee chose two primary information-gathering activities: a review of the existing literature on programs and policies designed to enhance female participation in S&E and site visits to four universities that had implemented successful approaches to advancing and retaining women students, faculty, or leadership as gauged by numbers of students and/or faculty. The goals of the site visits were

- to identify programs self-reported to be successful;
- to identify any original programs not already described in the literature;
- to observe programs in the context of a pathway analysis. (The committee approached the subject of recruiting and retaining women as a pathway that begins with postsecondary education and proceeds through graduate school, postdoctoral status, and into academic careers. Rather than focus on one level, the committee examined the vertical pathway by meeting with students, faculty, and administrators across the levels.);
- to add to current knowledge about programs to assist women; and
- to put a human face on the programs.

Equally important is what the study committee did not do. It did not review all programs at higher education institutions. Rather, the four research-intensive institutions—two public and two private—chosen for site visits had successfully advanced gender issues on their campuses (see the brief descriptions of these reputations in the next section). The committee members who participated in the site visits paid particular attention to the engineering programs at two of the universities, the computer science program at one university, and the life sciences programs at the fourth. Each of these institutions reported success in recruiting or retaining female students or faculty in S&E in the 1990s and during the time the committee selected the cases for study. This progress was evident in gender-related reports released by the universities, in the public press coverage of the policies and practices instituted by university administrators, and in the published statistics denoting increases in percentages of female students and faculty.

On three other dimensions, institutions were chosen with variation in mind. First, both private and public institutions were included. Public and private universities are constrained differently by state policies. For example, because of legal rulings many state universities no longer have targeted admissions strategies or offer race-specific scholarships. In response, some institutions have creatively increased the pool of candidates from which to admit students or have implemented programs designed to encourage attendance by women.

Second, both small and large institutions were chosen. The particular characteristics of a large versus a small department or school might play a role in the kinds of procedures or programs adopted. One university was classified as "large," having over 25,000 students. A second university was classified as "medium," with between 10,000 and 25,000 students.

The remaining two universities were "small," both with less than 10,000 students.

Third, universities were selected from different regions of the United States: two from the Midwest, one from the South, and one from the Northeast. Scholars have suggested that the location of an institution plays a role in the decisions of prospective faculty (Trower and Chait, 2002) and that geography plays an important role for women (Kulis and Sicotte, 2002). Institutions located in large metropolitan areas may not have to offer special incentives such as a spousal hiring program aimed at attracting the best faculty, whereas geographically isolated institutions that serve as a region's major employer might have to consider spousal employment for every faculty position search.

At the four institutions visited, the committee members met separately with department chairs, deans, top-level administrators (i.e., provost, chancellor, or president), women faculty, undergraduates, and graduate students. Although postdoctoral students were not the focus of these meetings—the National Academies' Committee on Science, Engineering, and Public Policy (COSEPUP) had recently completed a similar study specifically about those students (COSEPUP, 2000)—some discussion of postdocs was included in site visits. The goal of these meetings was to identify the range of policy responses adopted by these institutions that likely resulted in their general success in attracting and retaining women. Interviewees commented on various issues related to the recruitment and retention of women. The issues, for the most part, were those at the heart of the challenges to the universities that had necessitated their policy responses.

Several committee members went on each one-day site visit, which was divided into various meetings. Prior to the site visits, the committee agreed on the appropriate questions and topics to be discussed during the visits, and then sent the topics to each university before the visit itself. At the meetings, interviewees were encouraged both to discuss the themes and to bring up additional themes they felt were important. A consultant engaged by the committee took notes.

ADVANCING WOMEN: A SNAPSHOT OF THE FOUR INSTITUTIONS

All the universities visited have been able to increase their percentages of female students and faculty. The perception of administration officials is that the climate affecting the recruitment, retention, and advancement of women has improved as well. For example, among faculty at one university the progress had been rapid; women were holding more endowed chairs and full professorships. One-third of deans were women, which strengthened the female presence in promotion and tenure decisions. Over a decade one department added over 10 women faculty. In another department over half of the faculty members hired in the late 1990s were women. Finally, the computer science department of one of the institutions had the highest percentage of women faculty of any college or department of computing in the country.

Likewise, at another university, admissions statistics indicated that over the period that the computer science department began its efforts to recruit women students, the number of both male and female applicants to the undergraduate program rose steadily and a significantly higher proportion of women applicants were accepted each year. In addition, according to the office of admissions, standardized scores remained high (in 2001 the average math SAT I score for entering students was 760), and measures of outside achievement and personal attributes were at an all-time high.

Additional improvements were found in student retention. In 2000 there was "zero attrition" among women students between the freshman and sophomore years—traditionally a high dropout period. A dean attributed this situation in part to multiple entry points to computer programming and in part to attentive mentoring. Some interviewees suggested that an additional benefit was that the more diverse environment led to an improvement in pedagogy. Perhaps most important, according to a female dean, although the percentages have not changed much for graduate students and faculty, the culture has changed: "The undergraduates in computer science have energy and enthusiasm. The graduate women are part of that. There is a critical mass we've never seen before, and activism."

The universities visited also experienced positive changes in hiring practices. At one school, a dean put new search committee rules into effect to attract more women. At the time, the engineering school had five women faculty; in less than a decade that figure had quadrupled. The university's engineering school now has one of the highest percentages (over 10 percent) of women faculty among the major engineering schools.

This particular engineering school has also succeeded on several other fronts. During the 1990s the proportion of women in the engineering school earning Ph.D.'s grew from about 10 percent to almost 30 percent—the second highest among major engineering schools. Of the women earning engineering Ph.D.'s over a six-year period in the mid-1990s, 22 percent took faculty positions. Of minorities earning Ph.D.'s, 40 percent took faculty positions. Related to this result, this school of engineering has the third highest percentage of African American students among its peer institutions (nearly 9 percent) and one of the highest graduation rates (90 percent) of all engineering schools. Finally, overall at this institution the net retention rate for undergraduate women in the engineering program was about 100 percent—that is, women who drop out of the program tend to be replaced by transfers from other departments.

By way of an explanation, officials pointed to this institution's entrance standards, which are high for all applicants, and its strong support system. The increase in the percentages of women and minorities at this institution occurred at the same time that its engineering school was improving its recruitment and retention percentages. The school's overall rank among all U.S. engineering schools in the *U.S. News and World Report* rankings rose from below 35th in 1990 to the top 15 in 1998. Three of the school's engineering programs were ranked among the top five nationally, and five were ranked among the top 10.

All four of the institutions visited were major research universities. Research universities train most of the country's Ph.D.'s and perform a disproportionate amount of funded research. What happens to women in these institutions and what changes can be made to advance the careers of women while the universities simultaneously pursue their research missions can serve as a model for a range of higher education institutions. In addition, because women make up the smallest proportion of the science and engineering faculty in research universities, the methods used by successful institutions can indicate avenues for change in those organizational settings where it is needed most.

ORGANIZATION OF THE GUIDE

The guide is divided into seven chapters. Chapter 2 looks closely at the recruitment of women—of secondary students for postsecondary study in S&E, of undergraduates for graduate programs in S&E, and of postdoctorates for faculty positions. This chapter corresponds to the first, third, and fourth issues detailed in the study committee's charge. Chapter 3 examines the retention of female undergraduate and graduate students. It corresponds to the second and third issues in the charge. Chapter 4, which looks at ways to enhance the hiring of female faculty for assistant professor positions, takes up the third and fourth issues in the charge. Chapter 5 focuses on retaining female faculty—the fifth charge issue. And Chapter 6 examines efforts to increase the number of women in administrative positions—the final issue. The concluding chapter summarizes the main strategies.

Chapters 2-6 begin with a discussion of the challenges and obstacles facing women at specific stages of the higher education pathway. These chapters then examine the strategies undertaken by the four universities visited, as well as by other institutions, to remedy those challenges and overcome obstacles. Each chapter concludes with a "to do" list for faculty and administrators.

2

Recruiting Women Students

Recruitment of students into science and engineering (S&E) programs is an interactive process, reflecting the intersection of a university's efforts to enroll students and students' desires to attend a particular institution. Two assumptions underlie strategies designed to attract women to undergraduate and graduate education in S&E: first, the group of female S&E college applicants is larger than the number that actually enroll (i.e., there is a gap between interest and enrollment); and, second, following the first assumption, there are obstacles to recruiting additional women. Both of these assumptions emerged in the meetings held at the four universities visited. This chapter addresses the challenges confronting universities as they try to recruit more female undergraduates and graduates, and it examines the recruitment strategies adopted by the universities visited and other institutions.

CHALLENGES

In 2001 women comprised 48.9 percent of 20- to 24-year-olds and 49.3 percent of 25- to 29-year-olds in the United States (NSF, 2004c). Women are more likely than men to enroll in postsecondary education immediately after completing high school. In 2001, 64 percent of women—compared with 60 percent of men—did so (NSB, 2004). Women constitute a majority of undergraduate students, and many choose to major in S&E programs.

The two assumptions that underlie strategies designed to attract women to undergraduate and graduate education in S&E can be assessed by means of information that compares female high school students interested in S&E with female undergraduates in S&E. The working hypothesis is that while both groups are likely growing, the ratio of the former to the latter remains larger.

Undergraduates

Interest in S&E among high school students is clearly rising. According to recent data from the U.S. Department of Education (2004:70):

> Since the early 1980s, when states began to increase the number of required courses to receive a high school diploma, the percentage of high school graduates completing advanced coursework in science and mathematics has increased. In 1982, 35 percent of high school graduates had completed advanced science coursework (i.e., at least one course classified as more challenging than general biology); this percentage had increased to 63 percent by 2000. Most of this increase is attributable to increases in the rates at which graduates completed chemistry I and/or physics I because the percentage who had completed at least one course of either chemistry II, physics II, or advanced biology increased only from 15 to 18 percent between 1982 and 2000.

The percentage of high school graduates who had completed courses in advanced academic mathematics (i.e., completed at least one course classified as more challenging than algebra II and geometry I) increased from 26 percent in 1982 to 45 percent in 2000. Moreover, the percentage that had completed advanced level II (i.e., precalculus or an introduction to analysis) more than tripled (from 5 percent to 18 percent). The percentage that had completed advanced level III (i.e., a course in calculus) doubled (from 6 percent to 13 percent).

Female students' interest in science, as reflected in the percentages of male and female high school students taking math and science classes, has also increased (Table 2-1).

Women's interest in the lower-level mathematics classes has consistently been higher than that of male students, and has been growing. For the higher-level mathematics classes, women's participation has clearly grown, although the percentage of females taking these courses lags a bit behind the percentage of male students. Likewise, a greater percentage of women are taking biology and chemistry.

Additional evidence of female high school students' interest in S&E can be gleaned from the percentage of women taking advanced placement (AP) subject exams in high school. In general, women are more likely to take AP exams than men: in 2004, 56.2 percent of AP participants were women (College Board, 2005). In selected fields, it is clear that women are quite interested in S&E (Table 2-2).

TABLE 2-1 Percentage of High School Graduates Taking Selected Mathematics and Science Courses in High School, by Sex: 1990, 1994, and 1998

Course	1990			1994			1998		
	Total	Male	Female	Total	Male	Female	Total	Male	Female
Mathematics									
Geometry	63.2	62.1	64.2	70.0	64.3	72.2	75.1	73.7	77.3
Algebra II	52.9	51.0	54.6	61.1	57.7	61.6	61.7	59.8	63.7
Trigonometry	9.6	9.8	9.4	11.7	11.1	12.3	8.9	8.2	9.7
Precalculus	13.4	14.0	12.8	17.3	16.3	18.3	23.1	23.0	22.9
Calculus	6.5	7.5	5.6	9.3	9.5	9.1	11.0	11.2	10.6
Science									
Biology	90.9	89.4	92.3	93.2	91.8	94.5	92.7	91.4	94.1
AP/Honors Biology	10.1	9.4	10.8	11.9	10.9	12.8	16.2	14.5	18.0
Chemistry	48.9	47.7	50.0	55.8	52.9	58.5	60.4	57.1	63.5
Physics	21.5	25.4	18.0	24.5	27.0	22.2	28.8	31.7	26.2
Engineering	4.2	4.4	4.1	4.5	3.9	5.0	6.7	7.1	6.5

NOTES: Numbers have been revised from previously published figures. These data only report the percentage of students who earned credit in each course while in high school and do not count those students who took these courses prior to entering high school. Included in the totals but not shown separately are graduates whose sex was not reported.
SOURCE: NSF (2003:103).

TABLE 2-2 Percentage of AP Examinees Who Are Female, by Subject, 2004

Subject	Percentage of Examinees Who Are Female
Biology	58
Calculus AB	48
Calculus BC	40
Chemistry	46
Computer science A and AB	15
Physics B	35
Physics C	25
Statistics	50

SOURCE: NAE and NRC (2005).

Tables 2-1 and 2-2 suggest that a large and growing proportion of female secondary students appear to be interested in S&E.

Overall enrollments in both public and private secondary schools have risen over time, suggesting that greater numbers of females are enrolling in secondary education (US DOE, 2004). This finding should translate into greater numbers of women majoring in S&E as undergraduates.

Evidence for that conclusion can be found in the number of S&E baccalaureate degrees awarded to women (Figure 2-1). The number of

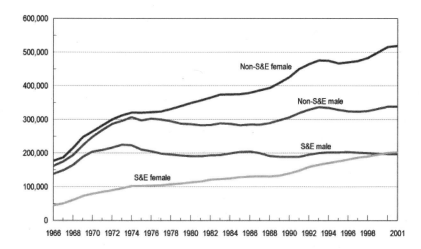

FIGURE 2-1 Number of baccalaureate degrees awarded, by field and gender, 1966-2001.
SOURCE: NSF (2004c).

TABLE 2-3 Percentage of Bachelor's Degrees
Awarded to Women, by Field, 2001

Field	Percent
All fields	57.4
S&E	50.6
Sciences	55.9
Biological/agricultural sciences	57.3
Computer sciences	27.6
Earth, atmospheric, and ocean sciences	40.9
Mathematics/statistics	48.0
Physical sciences	41.7
Psychology	77.5
Social sciences	54.8
Engineering	20.1
Non-S&E	60.5

SOURCE: NSF (2004c).

women receiving baccalaureate degrees in S&E has risen substantially and is now equal to or above the number of men.

Women and men pursue particular S&E disciplines to different extents. A greater portion of degrees in biological and agricultural sciences, psychology, and the social sciences went to women in 2001 (Table 2-3), whereas most degrees in engineering were awarded to men.

When the evidence of women's interest in S&E is compared with the intentions of college freshmen to major in S&E, one might expect many more female S&E majors. However, women's interest in majoring in S&E has not changed very much. The percentage of freshmen intending to major in S&E between 1977 and 2002 has risen (Table 2-4):

• For white females, the percentage has risen slightly since 1977, from about 20 percent to about 24 percent in 2002, but has dropped slightly from a high in the early 1990s.

• For Asian American females, the percentage has risen from about 30 percent to about 34 percent and, like the data for whites, is lower in 2002 than it was in the 1990s.

• For black females, there has been a noticeable increase from about 21 percent to about 33 percent.

• For Mexican American/Chicana and Puerto Rican American females, there has been an increase from about 25 percent to about 31 percent.

• For American Indian/Alaskan Native females, there has been a slight increase from about 26 percent to about 27 percent.

For all races or ethnicities, male freshmen are more likely than female freshmen to intend to major in S&E, generally defined, and in specific fields such as engineering. Female freshmen, however, are more likely than male freshmen to intend to major in biological and agricultural sciences along with social and behavioral sciences, regardless of race or ethnicity.

The proportion of women freshmen intending to major in S&E is fairly consistent across all S&E disciplines. More men are choosing computer science, whereas fewer men are choosing the physical sciences and the biological/agricultural sciences (Table 2-5). Women are increasingly choosing the biological/agricultural sciences, social/behavior sciences, and engineering over the physical sciences, mathematics/statistics, and computer sciences.

The combination of these data on high school interest in S&E, enrollment data, degree data, and freshmen interest in S&E suggests that more women are receiving degrees in S&E because the number of women attending postsecondary institutions—rather than the proportion of collegiate women interested in S&E—is rising. In fact, female freshmen are not much more interested in S&E than they used to be, nor has the distribution of women's interest in particular disciplines changed much. Women still prefer the biological sciences over engineering.

Ultimately, it is the student's decision to apply and enroll in a college program. One can simply portray this decision as a binary choice to pursue an S&E program in college or not. Universities are increasingly challenged in their recruiting efforts as prospective students see lower benefits or higher costs in pursuing an S&E degree. Some costs, such as paying for college, affect both male and female students.[1] However, other factors affect male and female students differently.

Two obstacles sometimes encountered in recruiting more women to undergraduate study in S&E are differences in preparation for such study and negative attitudes about S&E. As for differences in preparation, women face more of an uphill battle to succeed in an S&E program—not because of a difference in aptitude, but because they have to absorb more information in less time. Both men and women take S&E courses in high school, but there is a slight but important difference in the kinds of courses they take. Women are more likely to take mathematics courses

---

[1]For example, if S&E degrees take longer to achieve than non-S&E degrees, students concerned about financing college might be tempted to enroll in non-S&E programs.

TABLE 2-4 Freshmen Intending to Major in S&E, by Race/Ethnicity, Sex, and Field: Selected Years, 1977-2002 (percentage distribution)

Race and Ethnicity/Sex/Field	1977	1981	1984
White	30.0	32.7	32.8
Men	39.5	43.9	42.9
Physical sciences	4.5	3.8	3.2
Biological/agricultural sciences	8.2	6.7	6.3
Mathematics/statistics	1.3	0.9	1.1
Computer sciences	2.1	7.2	6.5
Social/behavioral sciences	6.6	5.8	6.3
Engineering	16.8	19.5	19.5
Women	20.3	22.5	23.2
Physical sciences	1.5	1.3	1.3
Biological/agricultural sciences	6.2	4.8	5.0
Mathematics/statistics	1.1	1.0	1.3
Computer sciences	1.2	4.5	3.0
Social/behavioral sciences	8.4	7.6	9.2
Engineering	1.9	3.3	3.4
Asian American	43.1	49.4	49.6
Men	55.6	60.7	61.0
Physical sciences	6.3	5.4	5.2
Biological/agricultural sciences	10.0	7.9	10.9
Mathematics/statistics	1.6	1.2	1.1
Computer sciences	3.5	6.3	6.1
Social/behavioral sciences	4.5	3.4	5.1
Engineering	29.7	36.5	32.6
Women	29.8	37.2	37.9
Physical sciences	3.4	2.7	3.2
Biological/agricultural sciences	9.3	9.2	10.6
Mathematics/statistics	1.3	1.6	1.2
Computer sciences	3.6	7.2	5.6
Social/behavioral sciences	7.0	7.0	6.9
Engineering	5.2	9.5	10.4
African American	26.5	33.0	30.9
Men	34.7	40.5	37.0
Physical sciences	2.0	1.6	1.1
Biological/agricultural sciences	5.2	4.1	5.0
Mathematics/statistics	0.7	0.8	0.5
Computer sciences	2.7	10.5	10.5
Social/behavioral sciences	9.0	6.0	7.1
Engineering	15.1	17.5	12.8
Women	20.8	27.9	26.8
Physical sciences	0.9	1.0	0.9
Biological/agricultural sciences	3.8	3.8	4.9
Mathematics/statistics	0.7	0.8	0.7
Computer sciences	1.9	9.3	8.9
Social/behavioral sciences	11.1	8.3	7.6
Engineering	2.4	4.7	3.8

1987	1990	1993	1996	1999	2002
27.8	29.3	31.7	32.3	31.7	31.3
35.6	37.3	39.8	40.4	40.0	39.6
2.8	3.2	3.3	2.7	2.4	2.8
5.3	5.8	8.1	8.4	7.1	6.2
1.0	1.0	0.9	0.8	0.7	0.9
3.3	2.9	3.2	5.6	7.7	5.5
7.0	7.6	7.6	6.7	6.3	7.2
16.2	16.8	16.7	16.2	15.8	17.0
20.9	22.7	25.2	25.7	24.9	23.9
1.2	1.3	2.0	1.6	1.6	1.5
4.3	4.9	7.3	9.3	8.8	7.6
0.9	0.8	0.7	0.7	0.6	0.7
0.9	0.9	0.6	0.8	1.1	0.5
11.2	11.9	11.2	10.5	10.4	11.1
2.4	2.9	3.4	2.8	2.4	2.5
47.5	42.8	42.8	48.0	47.5	43.2
56.0	52.7	51.1	58.0	60.0	55.0
3.2	3.4	2.8	2.0	2.0	2.2
11.1	10.9	13.4	11.3	8.9	10.2
0.7	1.0	0.6	0.7	0.6	0.9
4.6	4.3	4.2	11.6	19.4	8.1
5.4	6.6	6.5	4.3	4.8	6.1
31.0	26.5	23.6	28.1	24.3	27.5
38.1	33.2	34.5	37.5	35.9	33.5
2.4	1.6	2.2	2.3	1.4	1.6
13.0	9.4	13.5	14.1	13.3	13.5
1.2	0.8	0.8	0.6	0.6	0.8
2.6	1.8	1.4	3.4	6.2	1.6
11.3	12.2	10.7	10.0	8.5	9.9
7.6	7.4	5.9	7.1	5.9	6.1
31.0	31.5	37.9	36.9	37.2	35.4
36.8	35.1	44.6	40.8	41.7	40.2
1.3	1.2	2.0	1.2	1.4	1.3
4.1	4.5	6.8	6.6	5.8	5.8
0.7	0.4	0.6	0.5	0.6	0.4
6.3	6.7	6.6	8.8	13.2	8.2
6.9	7.5	7.4	6.2	7.4	8.0
17.5	14.8	21.2	17.5	13.3	16.5
26.8	29.6	34.0	34.3	34.0	32.5
0.9	0.7	1.7	1.5	1.0	1.3
3.9	5.0	7.8	9.9	9.2	10.0
0.6	0.5	0.6	0.6	0.6	0.5
4.4	5.1	4.6	5.0	5.3	2.5
11.2	13.4	11.7	12.5	13.8	14.5
5.8	4.9	7.6	4.8	4.1	3.7

continued

TABLE 2-4 Continued

Race and Ethnicity/Sex/Field	1977	1981	1984
Mexican American/Chicano and			
Puerto Rican American	31.7	36.4	33.8
Men	39.4	44.1	43.1
Physical sciences	1.7	3.0	2.5
Biological/agricultural sciences	6.1	7.0	6.1
Mathematics/statistics	1.7	0.6	0.6
Computer sciences	2.9	5.9	9.3
Social and behavioral sciences	10.9	5.4	7.5
Engineering	16.1	22.2	17.1
Women	24.6	28.9	25.7
Physical sciences	0.7	1.7	1.4
Biological/agricultural sciences	5.8	6.6	5.9
Mathematics/statistics	0.3	0.3	0.8
Computer sciences	2.6	5.8	5.6
Social/behavioral sciences	13.1	9.4	7.8
Engineering	2.1	5.1	4.2
Other Latino	NA	NA	NA
Men	NA	NA	NA
Physical sciences	NA	NA	NA
Biological/agricultural sciences	NA	NA	NA
Mathematics/statistics	NA	NA	NA
Computer sciences	NA	NA	NA
Social/behavioral sciences	NA	NA	NA
Engineering	NA	NA	NA
Women	NA	NA	NA
Physical sciences	NA	NA	NA
Biological/agricultural sciences	NA	NA	NA
Mathematics/statistics	NA	NA	NA
Computer sciences	NA	NA	NA
Social/behavioral sciences	NA	NA	NA
Engineering	NA	NA	NA
American Indian/Alaskan Native	32.7	30.0	29.6
Men	37.9	39.5	32.8
Physical sciences	3.8	3.2	1.1
Biological/agricultural sciences	9.1	5.8	8.3
Mathematics/statistics	2.4	0.7	0.1
Computer sciences	1.5	4.0	3.3
Social/behavioral sciences	9.3	6.2	6.0
Engineering	11.8	19.6	14.0
Women	25.8	16.4	22.3
Physical sciences	1.3	1.1	0.8
Biological/agricultural sciences	5.9	3.5	8.3
Mathematics/statistics	0.7	0.1	1.0
Computer sciences	1.3	1.4	2.6
Social/behavioral sciences	11.8	8.1	7.5
Engineering	4.8	2.2	2.1

NA = not available.
NOTE: The physical sciences include physics, chemistry, astronomy, and the earth, atmospheric, and ocean sciences.
SOURCE: NSB (2004:Appendix Table 2-6).

1987	1990	1993	1996	1999	2002
35.1	33.9	33.2	35.5	36.2	34.7
41.9	40.0	38.8	42.0	45.0	40.8
1.9	2.6	2.2	1.4	1.1	1.8
6.8	6.2	7.4	7.5	7.3	6.8
0.8	0.7	0.5	0.7	0.8	1.0
3.2	2.7	3.1	6.3	6.8	5.2
9.7	8.6	9.8	8.4	6.9	7.9
19.5	19.2	15.8	17.7	22.1	18.1
29.4	29.7	28.2	30.7	28.7	30.7
1.0	1.1	1.1	1.2	0.8	1.5
6.6	5.1	6.5	8.7	9.4	9.2
0.3	0.8	0.4	0.4	0.4	0.5
2.2	1.6	1.1	1.7	1.4	0.6
14.9	16.5	14.7	14.3	13.8	16.7
4.4	4.6	4.4	4.4	2.9	2.2
NA	NA	38.0	41.3	37.2	35.4
NA	NA	40.4	51.4	45.4	42.2
NA	NA	1.8	1.6	1.9	2.0
NA	NA	8.7	8.6	5.3	6.9
NA	NA	0.3	0.4	0.4	0.9
NA	NA	2.9	6.9	9.4	4.8
NA	NA	9.0	7.9	9.7	10.0
NA	NA	17.7	26.0	18.7	17.6
NA	NA	35.4	32.2	31.3	31.1
NA	NA	2.0	1.1	1.1	1.5
NA	NA	9.9	7.8	9.4	8.3
NA	NA	0.2	0.4	0.3	0.6
NA	NA	1.5	1.8	1.7	0.9
NA	NA	17.0	14.9	15.5	16.6
NA	NA	4.8	6.2	3.3	3.2
31.5	31.8	31.9	33.6	35.4	32.0
39.7	35.8	35.9	40.1	39.0	36.8
3.6	4.9	2.0	3.0	2.9	2.2
7.2	7.4	9.5	8.1	7.9	5.3
0.8	0.9	0.8	0.6	0.7	0.8
2.6	1.3	1.9	5.5	5.4	4.0
7.2	7.3	8.2	7.7	7.0	8.6
18.3	14.0	13.5	15.2	15.1	15.9
23.4	26.2	26.5	27.8	30.0	27.2
0.9	1.7	1.0	2.2	2.4	1.4
5.6	7.5	6.7	9.3	10.4	8.8
1.2	0.1	0.6	0.4	0.5	0.4
0.7	1.1	1.6	1.2	1.3	0.5
11.3	12.4	12.4	11.4	12.7	13.3
3.7	3.4	4.2	3.3	2.7	2.8

TABLE 2-5 Freshmen Intending to Major in S&E, by Sex and Field: Selected Years, 1977-2002 (percentage distribution)

Sex/Field	1977	1981	1984	1987	1990	1993	1996	1999	2002
Men	100.0	100.0	100.0	100.0	100.0	100.0	100.0	100.0	100.0
Physical sciences	10.3	7.9	6.9	7.0	7.4	7.5	5.9	5.4	5.9
Biological/agricultural sciences	20.1	15.1	14.8	14.8	15.6	20.4	18.4	15.5	15.0
Mathematics/statistics	3.2	2.2	2.5	2.4	2.4	2.0	1.8	1.8	2.2
Computer sciences	5.5	16.9	16.1	9.7	8.8	8.5	15.5	21.9	14.6
Social/behavioral sciences	17.5	13.0	14.9	19.7	20.5	18.5	16.1	15.5	18.1
Engineering	43.0	44.9	44.8	46.4	45.4	42.9	42.4	39.9	44.0
Women	100.0	100.0	100.0	100.0	100.0	100.0	100.0	100.0	100.0
Physical sciences	7.3	5.9	5.3	4.9	5.1	6.9	6.2	5.4	5.7
Biological/agricultural sciences	28.8	20.1	21.7	21.1	21.0	28.2	32.6	32.0	31.1
Mathematics/statistics	5.0	4.2	5.2	3.8	3.4	2.8	2.5	2.3	2.6
Computer sciences	6.6	21.5	15.7	6.1	6.3	4.2	5.6	7.0	3.2
Social/behavioral sciences	42.4	33.3	37.3	51.0	50.5	43.5	40.7	42.3	45.8
Engineering	9.9	15.0	14.6	13.2	13.8	14.4	12.6	11.2	11.5

NOTE: Physical sciences include physics, chemistry, astronomy, and earth, atmospheric, and ocean sciences.
SOURCE: NSB (2004:Appendix Table 2-6).

such as geometry, algebra II, and trigonometry, whereas men are slightly more likely to take precalculus and calculus. Men tend to take more mathematics earlier in their education. This may give them an edge in preparation. Furthermore, men are more likely to take physics and engineering, whereas women are more likely to take biology and chemistry (NSF, 2003:Appendix Table 1-1).[2]

Other studies have suggested, however, that women are not underprepared compared with men. In its study of beginning postsecondary students, the U.S. Department of Education states: "The low S&E enrollment by women implies that a very stringent selection mechanism might be at work in S&E program entry. The selection mechanism—either by women themselves or by institutional forces or by a joint effect of both—probably filters out all but a small group of highly resilient women for S&E programs. These women who enter S&E fields are likely to have strong family support, high expectation, healthy self-confidence, and solid academic preparation" (US DOE, 2000:88). However, these students were successfully recruited. The challenge lies in recruiting other students—and they may have less preparation.

As for the second obstacle—negative attitudes toward S&E—women tend to have less interest, expectations for success, and confidence regarding S&E than men (Xie and Shauman, 2003). Therefore, they may perceive fewer benefits to S&E education and careers. In the past, the culture of S&E was male-dominated. Now, even though the field is more open to a more diverse set of students and practitioners, many young people still view S&E as something men do. According to data collected by the U.S. Department of Education for the year 2000, female 4th, 8th, and 12th graders were less likely than men to agree with the statements "I like mathematics" and "I am good at mathematics" (NSF, 2003). Similar results were found for the statement "I like science" and "I am good at science." Prospective female students also may hear stories about harassment, "glass ceilings," lower salaries, and the marginalization of women in college (i.e., being excluded from more powerful or relevant positions or organizations). Indeed, the satisfaction or the return on the investment that a female student expects to receive may be lower.

Graduate Students

Women are increasingly filling the graduate education ranks in S&E (Figure 2-2). Over the 1990s the number of women enrolled in U.S. gradu-

---

[2]Peter and Horn (2005) argue, however, that women have closed the math gap in the highest mathematics course taken.

26

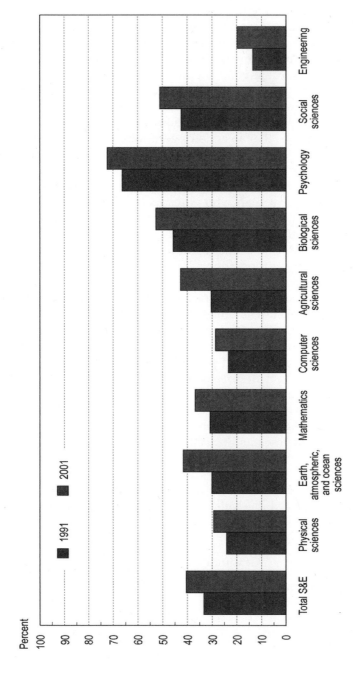

FIGURE 2-2 Female share of S&E graduate students, by field: 1991 and 2001.
SOURCE: NSF (2004c).

ate schools increased from 133,737 to 168,468, and the percentage of female graduate students in science and engineering increased from 34 percent to 41 percent (NSF, 2003). And like undergraduates, women are not distributed evenly across all S&E fields.

A significant drop-off, however, may occur between the number of women who receive a baccalaureate degree and the number who enroll in a graduate program. The numbers and percentages fall off with each successively higher degree (Figure 2-3). The gap between bachelor's degrees and master's degrees appears to have narrowed somewhat over the past 35 years; but overall the number of women who receive master's or doctoral degrees do not seem to be closing in on the level for women receiving bachelor's degrees (Figure 2-4).

Many students—both men and women—choose to go into employment, rather than continue in higher education after receiving their bachelor's degrees. Some evidence suggests that women are no more likely to leave the pathway than are men. According to the National Science Foundation (NSF), "Longitudinal data show that there is no more attrition for female bachelor's degree recipients—regardless of degree field—than for males between baccalaureate receipt and graduate enrollment. Among S&E bachelor's degree recipients, women are more likely than men to pursue additional study. In 1999, 33 percent of the women and 28 percent of the men who had received an S&E baccalaureate in academic year 1996-1997 or 1997-1998 were enrolled in an educational program either full or part time" (NSF, 2003:35).

At the graduate level, at least three challenges confront present efforts to enhance recruitment of women: departmental culture, a lack of female-friendly policies, and negative attitudes toward graduate education or career. As for departmental culture, most prospective female graduate students are fresh from the experiences of their undergraduate programs, which may bolster their views of marginalization, particularly in advanced undergraduate coursework. The male professors who dominate S&E departments may feel more comfortable working with male graduate students. Both male faculty and male graduates may unintentionally signal to women candidates that they would be less welcome.

Family-friendly policies are important for graduate students, especially for women who did not begin graduate school immediately after receiving a baccalaureate degree. Time spent on graduate study outside of the classroom is much more demanding and much more likely to be both during and outside the nine-to-five time frame. At this stage of their education, women, as the primary caregivers, begin to face the work-family conflicts so often described in the context of faculty women.

Finally, women may have a negative view of graduate education or career. Women may be less comfortable, and be less interested, in areas

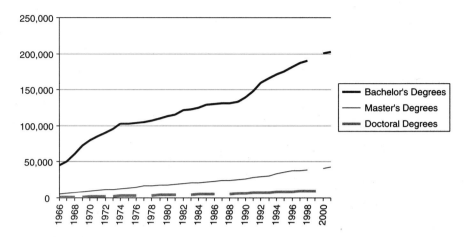

FIGURE 2-3 Number of women receiving bachelor's degrees, master's degrees, and doctoral degrees in science and engineering, 1966-2001. NOTE: Data for 1999 unavailable.
SOURCE: NSF (2004b).

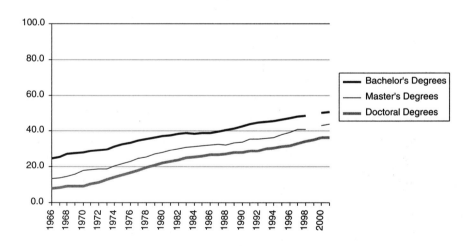

FIGURE 2-4 Percentage of women receiving bachelor's degrees, master's degrees, and doctoral degrees in science and engineering, 1966-2001. NOTE: Data for 1999 unavailable.
SOURCE: NSF (2004b).

that are primarily seen as "male," a view that may be reinforced in a prospective female graduate student when visiting a campus where no faculty members in the department of interest are female, and there are few female graduates. An additional challenge for graduate recruiting lies in the potential for employment for individuals with baccalaureate degrees. Women and men with bachelor's degrees may question the value of continued education.

Postdocs

The number of postdoctoral positions in S&E has increased over time (Figure 2-5). In 1979 postdoctoral men outnumbered women by a ratio of about four to one. By 2002 that ratio had dropped to about two to one. In 1979 women made up about 18 percent of all postdocs, but by 2002 that number had risen to about 34 percent.

Four factors may explain the slightly greater drop in females becoming postdocs, relative to females receiving Ph.D.'s: (1) insufficient advising or mentoring during the graduate program; (2) negative experiences during the graduate program; (3) individual preferences about career goals and views on the relevance of higher education; and (4) biases against female applicants for postdoctoral positions.

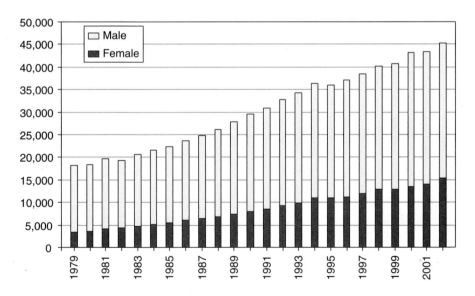

FIGURE 2-5 Postdocs in science and engineering, by gender, 1979-2002.
SOURCE: NSF, WebCASPAR.

A fuller discussion of challenges for postdocs in general is presented in the National Research Council publication, *Enhancing the Postdoctoral Experience for Scientists and Engineers: A Guide for Postdoctoral Scholars, Advisers, Institutions, Funding Organizations, and Disciplinary Societies.*

BOX 2-1
Summary of Challenges

Undergraduate Recruiting
✓ Female students are less likely to take higher levels of mathematics prior to enrolling in college and are more likely to concentrate on the biological sciences or chemistry.
✓ Female students have a less positive view of science and mathematics.

Graduate Recruiting
✓ Departmental cultures are more of an obstacle for women than for men.
✓ Universities often lack female-friendly policies.
✓ Students have negative perceptions of academic careers.

Postdoctoral Recruiting
✓ Universities provide insufficient advising and mentoring during the graduate program.
✓ Postdocs had negative experiences during their graduate careers.
✓ Postdocs have individual preferences about career goals and views on the relevance of higher education.
✓ There may be bias against female postdoctoral candidates.

RECRUITMENT STRATEGIES

Undergraduate Student Recruitment

In general, three principal strategies are used to recruit greater numbers of female undergraduate students: increasing preparation in secondary school, replacing the negative views and attitudes about S&E education (and careers) with positive ones, and creating a more female-friendly educational environment. Recruitment efforts are very important at the undergraduate level, because this is the beginning of the S&E pipeline that leads to employment as a scientist or engineer (including in academia as a faculty member).

The approaches adopted by institutions that have enjoyed success in bringing women into science and engineering include introducing previously unconsidered disciplines to potential students, acclimating students to science, engineering, and college-level academics, and altering the curricular and admission characteristics to fit the needs of new students.

BOX 2-2
Undergraduate Recruitment Strategies

✓ Have the institution signal the importance of women.
✓ Enhance science, engineering, and mathematics education at the K-12 level.
✓ Reach out to students at the K-12 level.
✓ Develop better methods for identifying prospective students.
✓ Create alternative assessment methods for admissions.
✓ Organize/improve on-campus orientations.
✓ Develop bridging programs.

Long-standing programs have evolved with successive iterations. The four institutions visited found that the introduction and success of a program often led to the development of another program that met different needs, which, in turn, led to still greater percentages of women. The programs and curricula often had feedback/feed-forward effects.

At each point of the undergraduate degree process—the period prior to enrollment in college, introduction to college-level academics, declaration of a major, undergraduate research, consideration of career path—the programs had the same general themes, although the execution or deployment of concepts varied at different institutions. Actions taken by different members of the academic institution, from undergraduate students up to the provost and president, had significant impacts at each of these points.

Some institutions took a comprehensive approach to recruiting women, starting with outreach programs for K-12 students, recruiting events for prospective undergraduate students, and targeted efforts to retain women students through graduation. Some programs became very elaborate and large; others maintained a small, more informal atmosphere. At times, outreach programs proved to be beneficial to the institution in ways beyond just recruiting female students. Elementary school outreach programs, for example, promoted good relations with the local community, which is positive for public institutions.

Approaches adopted by the four universities ranged from those fairly low cost (several thousand dollars for student-run programs) to those with significant costs (a women in science and technology program incorporating a designated women's dormitory and a dedicated class section with teaching assistant, faculty, and administrative coordinators). Some actions, such as facilitating increased interaction between students and faculty, cost almost nothing and yet can have large impacts.

Signaling the Importance of Women

At the institutional level, many different indicators, both direct and indirect, can set the climate and signal that the institution as a whole is committed to valuing and recruiting women. For prospective undergraduate students, an obvious indication is the willingness to commit significant resources to supporting women students such as dedicated space in a dormitory for women students in science and engineering. Presidents, provosts, and deans can demonstrate their commitment to encouraging a diverse student body—including women—through their speeches, conversations, and writings. Top-level administrators can also set targets for diversity to encourage recruitment. Both top administrators and chairs should meet with students.

Institutional signals need not require a substantial commitment of resources. One university moved the office of the program for women in engineering next to that of the dean of engineering. This uncomplicated move accomplished several things: it brought visibility and status to the program because of its proximity to the dean's office; it increased interaction between the dean's office staff and the program staff, facilitating collaboration on events; and it kept the issue of women in engineering in the forefront, less likely to be overlooked in the multitude of tasks facing the dean.

Indirectly, campuses can take various steps to show support for women on campus. One approach is establishing a committee on the status of women, including those who are undergraduate students. At one institution visited, the president formed and chaired a diversity advisory council and made a personal commitment to its activities. The council organized a campus-wide survey on gender issues and created several working groups to look at different aspects of diversity. An initial assessment concluded that the university was not promoting diversity, and the council made recommendations accordingly. Because the council had broad representation from across the campus, the recommendations were viewed as coming from the community rather than as an edict from above. The working groups monitored the success of specific practices implemented by a particular department or college, so that the successful practices could be used as models by colleagues in other departments. Incentive mechanisms also were developed at various levels. Central to the success of the effort were the accountability mechanisms put in place. For example, each department reported its diversity plan to its dean, who reported it to the council. Departments were therefore able to discuss issues and compare activities. Such committees exist at many higher education institutions. They indirectly improve the climate on campus and may make it easier to recruit women into S&E majors.

In summary, institutional signaling can be demonstrated through

- communications from top administrators;
- highlighting gender inclusiveness as a goal of the institution;
- creating an office or committee charged with promoting gender inclusiveness; and
- monitoring student concerns through such things as climate surveys and focus groups.

Enhancing S&E Education and Outreach Efforts at the K-12 Level

One theme that resonates throughout this guide is the idea that the education-to-career pathway is interconnected, and that improvements at earlier stages can lead to improvements at later ones. One way to convince more women (and men) to enter science and engineering at the university level is by enhancing and improving S&E education at the elementary and secondary levels. Universities can play a role in such an effort for several reasons. First, they may have a much clearer idea of what skills employers want. Teaching those skills requires certain prerequisites. Universities can help secondary schools to develop the appropriate curricula.

Second, universities teach secondary teachers. For example, one institution visited approached the gatekeepers—high school teachers—who could identify good students interested in computer science and direct them to university. Prompted by impending revisions in an advanced placement computer science exam, the National Science Foundation issued a call for proposals to prepare high school teachers for the change. A dean saw a recruiting opportunity and planned a program with dual objectives: to prepare high school teachers for the advanced placement change and, simultaneously, to discuss gender gap issues with them. The result was a summer institute attended by about 16 percent of all advanced placement high school teachers in computer science in the United States. The teachers that participated learned about the need for more women in computer science and the enthusiasm of this university to recruit them. As a result, the percentage of women entering the university's computer science program increased to 18 percent during a four-year period.

Examples of programs from schools not visited include project ASPIRE (Alabama Supercomputing Program to Inspire Computational Research in Education). This program "provides 1-week and 2-week professional development programs for high school and middle school teachers to help them instruct students in solving problems using a computational science approach to problem solving" (US DOE, 2001). EQUALS, a similar project, is also directed at educators at the K-12 level, in this case to enhance mathematics courses (US DOE, 2001). Overall, elementary and secondary school teachers can view universities and colleges as a valuable resource.

Aside from curricular issues and teacher preparation, secondary education must do everything it can do to combat the perception that S&E is something that only men do. Universities can assist secondary teachers by offering counterexamples: their own female students, who should be tapped to give presentations—along with female faculty—to secondary students.

Third, universities have developed various outreach efforts to enter the world of secondary students. The programs and efforts used to introduce K-12 graders to science and engineering are quite varied. They extend from programs that are simple, short term, and low cost, to those which are lengthy and require significant time and institutional resources. A coordinated series of events allows a department or college to offer outreach to students from kindergarten through high school. Some of the programs developed to increase children's interest in science and engineering have even received national attention.[3]

Career day events at local schools are venues for introducing science and engineering research problems to students who, throughout their school years, may not have been exposed to such projects nor have had an opportunity to interact with scientists and engineers. These events are most successful when they have a demonstrated objective and some application to real-world problems. For the younger grades, toys that demonstrate scientific principles are used successfully. For older students, a visit to the university or college can be the basis of an interest in science.

On one of the site visits, a department chair described how faculty from his department went into the elementary schools on a Saturday to talk to groups of fourth graders, parents, and teachers about engineering. They spiced up their presentations with demonstrations of small rockets, Jiggle Jelly, and other tools of interest to youngsters. Later they offered a day on engineering for female high school students, taught by female engineering graduate students.

These strategies suggest that universities can help elementary and secondary education institutions to improve the quality of their S&E education, reach more women, and combat negative views about women in science and engineering by

---

[3]The National Science Foundation's Program for Gender Equity has funded various efforts to elicit interest from K-12 girls in science and engineering. Information about these programs is available at http://www.nsf.gov.

- including respect for diversity in science teacher training;
- offering a resource to elementary and secondary schools, which want to ensure that course and ancillary materials present a positive picture of women in S&E; and
- having female college students and faculty interact with secondary students by means of visits, guest lectures, and judging science fairs, among other things. Alumni can also be an outreach resource.

Broadening the Search for Applicants

Higher education institutions must make sure that they are not missing any potential S&E undergraduates. As noted earlier, one strategy for doing so is to form connections with secondary schools from which the potential undergraduates would be drawn. Two other pools of students are transfer and returning students who have interrupted their education.

Transfer students enter a college or university from another institution such as a community college or another four-year institution.[4] But students may not transfer into the freshmen level. For example, students transferring from a community college may possess an A.S. degree and may transfer into a four-year institution as juniors. To successfully recruit students already enrolled in a postsecondary institution, institutions must form connections with one another. These connections may be formal articulation agreements or informal relationships between engineering faculty at a community college and at a neighboring four-year institution (NAE and NRC, 2005).

A second group of prospective students comes from the pool of candidates who finish secondary school and then halt their education for a period of time. Universities cannot identify these potential students by simply peering into secondary institutions. Some strategies used by universities to identify these students include

- outreach activities to community colleges, including visits and lectures by four-year faculty, coordination of curricula, and the establishment of transfer offices at four-year institutions;
- articulation agreements to encourage the transfer of community college students (including women) to four-year institutions; and

---

[4]According to data from NSF's National Survey of Recent College Graduates 2001, 47 percent of women with bachelor's or master's degrees in S&E had attended a community college compared with 41 percent of men (based on weighted data taken from NSF's SESTAT database on March 17, 2005; a table was constructed of the count for each "gender" by "attended community college").

- outreach to high school students who do not go immediately into college programs.

Revising the Admissions Process

One way to recruit a greater number of female undergraduates is to consider a broader range of factors in deciding on admissions and to reexamine the gatekeeper requirements. One university's computer science program required all incoming students to have prior programming experience for admittance to the program, something women were less likely to have. The dean examined data for the institution and concluded that prior experience in programming and related skills were not correlated with future academic performance, thus programming experience should not dominate the admissions criteria for computer science majors.

Any discussion of entry into programs immediately raises the specter of lowered admissions criteria and a dilution of the quality of admitted students. However, the institutions visited, rather than experiencing a diminution in student quality, found that the quality of students increased. At these institutions, admissions standards were not "lowered" in the traditional sense of the word, but examined to determine how they contributed to student quality and success in the program.

Organizing On-Campus Orientation

At another university visited, an early dean's decision to promote the participation of minorities and women in engineering led to a career day for middle and high school girls, a novel approach at the time. By 1980 the total engineering enrollment was 25 percent women and 12 percent African American, higher than the national average.

Many of this university's departments devoted generous portions of their budgets to bringing prospective graduate students for weekend visits, including hotel stays. Prospective students were encouraged to spend a lot of time with women graduate students during visits.

Finally, the school worked closely with the Society of Women Engineers in various activities, including a Career Day for Girls, a Bring Your Daughter to Work Day, and a Women Professionals from Industry program. At such recruiting events, female students can play an important role in the recruitment of prospective female students by voicing their views on the school's climate and curriculum.

One of the colleges of engineering visited brought 140 middle school students to campus for one week to interest them in careers in S&E. Another program, modeled on Upward Bound, brought in female and minority students from grades 9-12 who may have been talented but were disadvantaged in math and science. The program sponsored a mentor for them in their own schools. A summer engineering program offered sophomore and junior high school women and minorities several weeks of exposure to university faculty and students. This program has been successful; more than 30 percent of attendees have enrolled at the university. Yet another program begins by bringing sixth-graders to campus in groups from the same city. By bringing the students back each year, the university hoped they will form a cohesive group and eventually enroll in the university's science and engineering program. According to the dean of engineering, successful programs are those that stress repeated experiences and interaction with inspiring faculty.

The president of one university decided to promote special events to recruit diverse undergraduate students. In what has become a longtime special event, several hundred female, African American, and Asian students are invited to spend the weekend on campus to meet with current students and faculty and to visit labs and other areas. The immediate goal of the university in initiating the program was to increase the female S&E student population. Such programs may be very useful for highly qualified applicants who are able to choose among many undergraduate institutions.

To nurture and sustain initial interest and present more in-depth views of science and engineering, some institutions have opted for longer events. These can take the form of a week-long "camp," incorporating different areas of science or engineering, or multi-week sessions, typically held during the summer. These events familiarize students with science and engineering topics. An example of a summer camp from a school (not visited) was a week-long mathematics camp held twice, in 1999 and 2000, by the Department of Mathematics at the University of Southern Colorado. Chacon and Soto-Johnson (2003) note that the process of holding the camp involved, among other steps, identifying the purpose of the camp; securing funding; determining course curriculum; identifying and planning ancillary activities; identifying instructors; identifying who would be invited to participate, how the admissions process would work, and how prospective invitees would be located; and program evaluation.

In a similar effort, the chair of an engineering institute at one of the institutions visited brought high school and middle school students, as well as college freshmen, to the institute for a hands-on, week-long camp focusing on robotics and featuring LEGOs, motors, computers, and other devices. The students worked with PowerPoint presentations and a web site, set up contests, and watched demonstrations.

Most programs of this type center on an on-site visit, meetings with faculty and graduates of the program, visits to labs that offer demonstration projects, and interaction with students. These events are designed to pique the interest of students who are considering attending the institution. Such events are also geared toward identifying students who may not have considered pursuing a degree in science or engineering or who have never been introduced to the concept of pursuing science and engineering as a career. These programs address the following critical issues:

• Many middle and high school students have never been in a research lab and do not know what goes on in "research."
• An introduction to women faculty drives home the point that women are experts in technical fields.
• Interaction with current students and degree graduates demonstrates the different levels of success possible. Younger students can more easily identify with speakers closer to their age than with senior faculty.
• Giving women undergraduate and graduate students the opportunity to teach younger students or K-12 teachers about their discipline helps these student feel that their knowledge is useful, which is highly motivating for them.

These events are most frequently hosted by a department or a college, because they can offer a range of lab visits and demonstration projects. The events do not need to be costly, nor do they always require a significant faculty or administration presence in the organization. One of the most successful events was hosted by a student organization at one of the universities visited. The organization recruited all of the speakers and the participants in demonstration projects (e.g., students and faculty) and undertook outreach to local high schools. The limited financial outlay was provided by the dean of engineering. Some events even included parents, offering them parallel programming so that students and parents could meet separately with university representatives.

On-campus orientations complement outreach efforts: instead of going to the secondary schools, the secondary students are brought to campus. Specific strategies have taken a number of forms, including

• science and engineering competitions or contests;
• visits with students and faculty;
• visits to labs or allowing prospective students to use major equipment such as telescopes or a scanning electron microscope;
• career day; and
• "bring your daughter to work day."

The length of strategies has also varied: day visits, weekend visits, or week-long or longer programs.

Developing Bridging Programs

Bridging programs are held in the summer for students who have just graduated from high school and are preparing to enter a university or college in the fall. Such programs are intended to acclimatize students to the college level and to offer then a chance to brush up on certain subjects—all to ease the transition from high school to college. Bridging programs serve two primary functions: orientation and a jump-start on education. An example of a related program is a student exchange program between Princeton University and Smith College (the nation's first women's college to have an engineering school). Designed for juniors, the exchange program is designed to help students succeed in graduate school and in engineering careers (Anonymous, 2005).

Graduate Student Recruitment

Because graduate students are recruited at the departmental level, faculty advisers and departments play a much bigger role in the environment surrounding graduate students than surrounding undergraduate students. Indeed, the institutional setting for graduate students is in reality the department, and many aspects of graduate student training and life, such as stipends, may vary from department to department. Some disciplines follow a certain pattern of training and curriculum, in which an incoming graduate student may undertake a series of rotations through various faculty labs before choosing one in which to pursue a thesis. The process of qualifying examinations from the master's to doctoral level, the thesis proposal defense, and the thesis committee composition requirements all may vary from department to department, even within the same school at a university. Within this setting, those at the highest levels in the institution must establish an environment supportive of women. Better academic preparation is less of a concern for graduate students

---

BOX 2-3
Graduate Student Recruitment Strategies

✓ Have the institution and S&E departments signal the importance of recruiting women.

✓ Enhance science, engineering, and mathematics education at the undergraduate level.

✓ Develop better methods for identifying prospective students.

✓ Organize on-campus orientations.

✓ Offer financial aid.

---

than for undergraduate students. Rather, the focus is on combating any negative views or experiences of undergraduates toward further study in science and engineering. Universities are also competing with employers at this point. The overall goal for universities is to show female students that they can be capable scientists and engineers and that they would benefit from the additional educational experience.

Signaling the Importance of Women

The university as a parent institution can provide some general structure for graduate students such as uniform health insurance, housing, child care (if available), and parking. For most other things, graduate students look to their departments.

General approaches to improving the recruitment and retention of graduate students are implemented by an institution, but often it is the tone set by an administration that actually facilitates change. A dean of engineering who came from a position in industry was supportive and outspoken about the value of graduate women and minorities in science and engineering. The "national crisis" in scientific and engineering talent cannot be resolved, he pointed out, without educating more women and minorities. He then praised the decision in 2000 by the "Big Ten Plus" deans to quickly address the "pipeline problem" and to share best practices. According to the dean, the university's "industrial partners" are making it clear that they highly value diversity and want to see more women and minorities among university graduates. "If a company wants to sell a car to as many people as possible," he said, "they want a design team that represents all those people." A diverse workforce requires a diverse student body.

The role of the department chair in setting the tone of the department is also critical. A department chair can signal support in many ways, as was demonstrated at some of the institutions visited. The chair sets policy and procedure within the department and allocates resources to support various activities. The chair also has influence at various stages of the graduate program. Because graduate recruiting is conducted primarily at the department level, a chair can have a significant influence on how recruiting is conducted. For example, the chair can call for recruiting materials to be sent to a diverse group of universities and colleges. Likewise, the chair can encourage faculty to ask their colleagues at peer institutions to recommend diverse candidates for graduate study. During the degree program, the chair can decide what approach and tone will be adopted by the department when issues arise and provide support to activities aimed at helping women students. The chair can support and reinforce institutional policies on sexual harassment, provide funds for refreshments at a lunchtime seminar series or journal club, or support a group that simply gets together to network and mentor one another.

Finally, faculty support is important. As thesis advisers and lab directors, faculty members are central figures in the daily lives of graduate students. They set the conditions of work in the lab or research group, determine the funding stream, and supervise students' research. For many students the research group is also the center of social interaction and serves as their community. For this reason, faculty members, by setting the tone for the working environment, have more influence than anyone else. For faculty with less experience working with women graduate students, some issues that arise may not be anticipated. For example, personal safety issues may be different for women working alone at night in a lab. One faculty member commented that whereas general safety issues had been "background noise," as he put it, the issue of personal safety became a much higher priority when women students joined the lab. Similarly, safety issues also are a factor in housing arrangements for women; on-campus housing may be more important for women who may want to live closer to limit the distance to and from the lab at odd hours.

A final resource for departments interested in better reaching prospective female graduate students is the department's web site. "Departmental web sites are sometimes designed to emphasize the participation of women" (Whitten et al., 2003:253), which is an important step because the site may be the first entrée the student sees at an institution. According to Bozeman and Hughes (2004:243), "A glance at the photographs on the web site of any large U.S. mathematics department leads to an unmistakable conclusion: Almost all of the faces belong to men. Inevitably, there is a cluster of female faces, but these in all likelihood belong to the non-tenure-track faculty and staff members. From the vantage point of a student at a women's college or a minority-serving institution, this revelation is jarring." An additional measure is for departments to specifically reference the importance of diversity in admissions policies and practices (Cuny and Aspray, 2001).

Thus institutional signaling can take the form of

• communications from deans and department chairs about the importance of inclusiveness: use of the department's web site to inform women; departmental publications that promote inclusiveness—that is, include pictures of female students, faculty, or scientists;
• monitoring student concerns through climate surveys and meetings with students; and
• developing female-friendly or family-friendly policies to support students on issues such as campus security or child care.

Enhancing and Improving Undergraduate S&E Programs

Just as improvements in secondary school make it easier to recruit prospective undergraduates, improvements in women's experiences in undergraduate school make it easier for universities to recruit graduates. Strategies might entail establishing programs to give female S&E students greater access to research projects, which can better acclimate them to the kind of work expected in graduate school. In general, departments could encourage graduate students and faculty to work more with undergraduates. Steps taken by departments and institutions to combat any negative attitudes female students might have about continuing in higher education also would be helpful in recruiting women as well as men.

Identifying Prospective Students

Any efforts by faculty to advise undergraduates about the possibilities of going to graduate school and to bring especially talented undergraduates to the attention of departments would help graduate student recruitment. Bringing undergraduates together on campus for a conference hosted by the university, for example, also could be beneficial. In 2000, the Computing Research Association's Committee on the Status of Women in Computing Research held a workshop on recruiting and retaining women graduate students that echoed these points and is relevant to the range of S&E disciplines. The first recommendation of the workshop was to "broaden the recruitment pool beyond students with undergraduate CSE [computer science and engineering] majors" (Cuny and Aspray, 2001:3). "Students without traditional backgrounds can succeed—and indeed flourish—in CSE graduate programs. Departments should go beyond the traditional applicant pool to recruit and admit strong students without undergraduate degrees in CSE. The potential of such students can be judged on academic records, difficulty of electives, successful research experiences, leadership roles, involvement in computing-like activities in their work or volunteer efforts, and internship experiences" (p. 4).

Other recommendations from the Cuny and Aspray report suggest broadening the criteria used in admissions. Schools should also encourage the reentry of students who have interrupted their education. Schools would therefore have to think more broadly about the relevance of broader criteria for admissions such as work experience.

Organizing On-campus Orientations

In a review of enculturation practices at a large public research university, Boyle and Boice (1998:88) noted that "the departments that excel at enculturating graduate students supplement the general orientation [held by the institution] with a departmentally sponsored orientation. These departments realize that it is the departmental culture, not necessarily the university culture, to which their incoming students will need to adjust." Orientations could be held to introduce undergraduates to graduate students or faculty and to a department's labs and research projects. Orientation also could take the form of bridging programs, similar in purpose to those held between high school and the start of undergraduate education. Such programs could assess students' skills and procedures for remedying deficiencies such as reading lists and summer courses or mentoring (Cuny and Aspray, 2001).

Offering Financial Aid

Research assistantships are very valuable in promoting the careers of graduate students. Thus departments should ensure that they offer these positions in similar numbers to male and female candidates, and make the positions as flexible as possible. As one academic noted, "When graduate aid comes in the form of teaching assistantships, as it does in my university, there is far less flexibility for taking time off. That especially affects women" (Kerber, 2005).

Postdoctoral Recruiting

Postdoctoral recruitment and the recruitment of new, tenure-track assistant professors involve many of the same issues (see Chapter 4 for additional discussion). Although institutional policies such as child care are likely to be important to both postdocs and new junior faculty, the hiring for these positions is conducted differently.

BOX 2-4
Postdoctoral Recruitment Strategies

✓ Have the institution and S&E departments signal the importance of recruiting women.
✓ Enhance science, engineering, and mathematics education at the graduate level.
✓ Develop better methods for identifying prospective postdocs.
✓ Establish female- and family-friendly policies and practices.
✓ Increase postdoctoral salaries.

Signaling the Importance of Women

As with graduate students the university as a parent institution can provide some general structure for postdoctoral students such as uniform health insurance, housing, child care (if available), and parking. For most other things, postdoctoral students look to their departments, and especially their labs.

Approaches to improving the recruitment of postdoctoral students are implemented by an institution, and the tone set by an administration can facilitate change. A department chair can signal support in many ways, by setting policy and procedure within the department and allocating resources to support various activities.

Faculty support is paramount. Because postdoctoral recruiting is conducted primarily at the individual faculty or laboratory level, the role of the faculty member is critical. At this stage, faculty are no longer instructors and advisers but peers and colleagues. How postdoctoral students are treated informs the perceptions and preferences of all involved, such as the considerations extended to women graduate students. Faculty members set the conditions of work, determine the funding source, and guide postdoctoral research. The research group is the social center and community for the postdoc.

Another form of institutional signaling is creation of an organizational mechanism for oversight of departmental practices regarding postdocs. At a minimum, deans, provosts, and departmental chairs can remind the faculty involved in postdoctoral searches that one component of the search is diversity.

Because postdocs tend to be older than graduate students, they are likely to face the same kinds of challenges faced by junior faculty: two-body problem in finding jobs, child-bearing, family responsibilities, and financial issues.[5]

Enhancing and Improving the Graduate Experience

Just as improvements in undergraduate education facilitate recruitment for graduate school, improving the graduate experience for women can ease the transition for women from predoctoral status to postdoctoral status. The process of learning about postdoctoral positions is partly formal (e.g., advertisements in the journal *Science*) and partly informal. As a result—and perhaps more so than for junior faculty—women graduate

---

[5]Because postdocs were not a focus of this guide, readers are encouraged to refer to other reports that have addressed the postdoctoral experience in depth. See, for example, COSEPUP (2000), Davis (2005).

students need to engage in networking and plug into their S&E discipline. Moreover, having a well-known mentor or adviser is likely to improve dramatically the chances that a recent Ph.D. will land a postdoctoral position. Finally, women graduate students, as part of the process by which they earn a Ph.D., also need to obtain the skills that lab directors and other faculty desire in postdocs. Department chairs and faculty should encourage all graduate students to develop good research, management, grant-writing, organizational, and time management skills, and ensure that women and men receive such training or mentoring equally.

Identifying Prospective Students

Faculty should advise their graduates about the possibilities and benefits of postdoctoral appointments and bring especially talented graduates to the attention of departments.

Establishing Female- and Family-Friendly Policies and Practices

By adopting various institutional policies and practices, universities could make themselves more attractive to prospective postdocs of either gender. These policies and practices include:

• *Establishing parental leave policies and child care.* Postdocs should be eligible for such benefits, which are often given to faculty. A recent survey of postdocs found that 34 percent were raising children (Davis, 2005).
• *Instituting sexual harassment sensitivity programs.* During the site visits, many people pointed out that within each discipline certain academic departments have reputations for being receptive or not receptive to women. At each institution, the issue of sexual harassment was raised. Most institutions responded that they have policies against sexual harassment and programs designed to educate employees. To improve the climate of a department for current faculty and to aid in recruiting women faculty, some institutions have taken steps to combat sexual harassment. At some institutions the policies were buttressed by personal meetings with a dean or other member of the administration.
• *Instituting regular studies to determine the equity of salaries and resources.*
• *Offering housing subsidies and access to medical and dental benefits.* Sigma Xi recently conducted a multi-campus survey of postdocs, and the preliminary results suggested that housing costs are a particular burden for many postdocs because their host institutions tend to be concentrated in pricey areas. More than 46 percent of respondents work in one of the 15 most expensive cities in the United States. It helps that most of the mar-

ried postdocs (who, in all, constitute almost 70 percent of our sample) have spouses who are gainfully employed. On the flip side, at least 28 percent of the married postdocs do not have spouses bringing home a paycheck. The statistic is worse for international postdocs with spouses, 43 percent of whom do not work outside the home, in some cases because of visa restrictions. Of the many single-earner households, nearly half (49 percent) spend more than a third of their income on rent (Davis, 2005:7).

Today the costs of health care are quite high. It may not be well known that postdocs who receive independent funding may not be automatically eligible for health insurance. Postdocs also are seeking greater access to retirement benefits (Davis, 2005).

Increasing Postdoctoral Salaries

A majority of postdoctoral positions are federally funded, and the majority of those are funded by the National Institutes of Health (Brainard, 2005). According to Kreeger (2004:178), "The salary levels of the National Research Service Awards (NRSA) given by the U.S. National Institutes of Health (NIH) are being used as de facto guidelines by postdocs and their supporters in university administration in seeking pay rises. . . . Administrators both inside and outside the United States take note of the NRSA scales, but these are not official guidelines and have no teeth." One solution would be to set minimum salary standards at each institution. Universities could set postdoctoral salaries against peer institutions or consider the NRSA salary level as a minimum threshold. At a minimum, administrators could survey postdocs at their institutions to determine whether postdocs in similar positions are paid similarly or could make salary guidelines more transparent.

BOX 2-5
Summary of Strategies for Recruiting Women Undergraduate, Graduate, and Postdoctoral Students

What faculty can do:

- Advise and mentor prospective and current female undergraduate and graduate students and postdocs.
- Conduct outreach to K-12 institutions to help prepare women for college and to combat negative attitudes about the place of women in science and engineering.
- Network with faculty at community colleges and other four-year institutions to broaden the search for prospective recruits.
- Invite female students to participate in research opportunities.
- Participate in bridge programs, campus visits, lectures, and seminars.
- Broaden admission criteria and cast a wider net in recruiting students.

What department chairs can do:

- Create an image of the department as female friendly and feature this image in promotional materials and on the department's web site.
- Communicate with faculty about the importance of diversity in recruiting.
- Support and reinforce a faculty member's commitment to advising and encouraging female students and postdocs through service awards and recognition during tenure and promotion reviews.
- Monitor the allocation of resources to students and survey students' opinions.

What deans and provosts can do:

- Communicate with department chairs about the importance of diversity in recruiting.
- Sponsor competitions, contests, career days, bridge programs, campus orientations, and other efforts to bring prospective students to campus.
- Monitor departments' progress in increasing the percentage of female students and postdocs.
- Conduct school-wide assessments of status of women.

What presidents can do:

- Publicly state the institution's commitment to diversity and inclusiveness whenever possible.
- Create an institutional structure, such as a standing committee, to address diversity issues within the student body. Charge that committee with monitoring diversity across the institution and with making recommendations to increase diversity.
- Demonstrate the institution's commitment by meeting with female students and postdocs and devoting resources to programs that assist them.

3

Retaining Women Students

T he goal of any academic program is to move students through to the completion of their majors to graduation. However, some undergraduate students who were interested in science and engineering (S&E) in high school may decide not to pursue a degree in an S&E discipline or to switch out of an S&E major.[1] Of particular importance at the undergraduate level is the timely enrollment of students in prerequisite classes so that they face no obstacles to taking more specialized S&E curricula in their junior and senior years.

For graduate students, attrition may more often mean leaving graduate education rather than switching to another major, as undergraduates might do. The committee was most interested in how universities can retain students through to their doctorates, because this degree is a prerequisite for postdoctoral and faculty positions in academia. Graduate attrition can be dramatic. Although good national-level data are lacking, estimates place attrition from Ph.D. programs at between 30 and 50 percent (Denecke, 2004). Golde (2000:199) writes that doctoral student attrition rates "consistently range from 40 to 50%." A recent study of Ph.D. completion at Duke University found that the completion rate for graduates in the biological sciences was 73 percent—and only 60 percent in the

---

[1] The committee did not deal directly with the issue of undergraduate students dropping out of college, although many of the reasons listed could lead to this outcome. Additional reasons may include financial hardship or lack of overall preparation.

physical sciences and engineering (Siegel, 2005).[2] Other studies report similar findings (NRC, 1996). Attrition seems to occur in clusters. In general, about a third of all doctoral student attrition occurs in the first year; another third occurs before candidacy; and the final third occurs after candidacy (Golde, 1998).

The many opportunities for attrition were a concern at all of the universities visited. For many universities, attrition is the natural outcome of students searching for what they perceive to be their optimal fit. But when students drop out of S&E majors and yet prefer to remain in the S&E program, attrition may stem from curriculum issues (e.g., content, instructional techniques, and pedagogies), students' characteristics (e.g., their preparation, interests, and ambitions), or students' positive or negative experiences with teachers, advisers, parents, and peers.

CHALLENGES

Undergraduates

Attrition of interested S&E undergraduates is worrisome (Seymour and Hewitt, 1997). Does it mean that S&E fields are failing to engage the interest of top students? According to one study, both male and female top students drop out of science and engineering at high rates. For example, in biology only 33 percent of top freshman biology majors go on to graduate in that field; the comparable number in mathematics is only 24 percent (Schroeder, 1998).

Available evidence of attrition rates disaggregated by gender presents a mixed picture. One study of beginning postsecondary students conducted by the National Center for Education Statistics at the U.S. Department of Education (US DOE, 2000:ix) found that "female students in S&E programs did not fall behind in the pipeline; they actually did better than male students in degree completion and program switch. This finding suggests that although women are less likely than men to enter S&E, those women who do enter S&E fields are likely to do well. Further, among students enrolled in 4-year S&E programs in the first year of college, women tend to have strong family support, high expectation, healthy self-confidence, and solid academic preparation." Other studies, however, have found that women persist in engineering programs—that is, complete a baccalaureate degree—to a lower degree than men (Adelman, 1998). Seymour and Hewitt (1997:14), defining persistence as intending to graduate, found that students in science and engineering (excluding the

---

[2]The analysis was based on Ph.D. cohorts matriculating from fall 1991 through fall 1995. The figures are percentages of completion as of fall 2004.

social sciences) had a high rate of switching out of their intended S&E major into the humanities, social sciences, or other non-S&E majors. More specifically, about 63 percent of freshman who declared the intent to major in mathematics or statistics switched to a non-S&E major. Seymour and Hewitt (1997:19) also found that "women more commonly than men switched to a major outside the group of their choice." However, the results in S&E are mixed: Seymour and Hewitt found that in engineering the switching rates for men and women were similar, whereas in the physical sciences men switch more than women. The authors conclude, though, that women leave S&E at a higher proportion than men.

One view is that, among top students, women are somewhat less likely to persist in S&E majors than men. The numbers in engineering are striking: "Only 29% of top undergraduate women remained in that major, compared with 82% of top undergraduate men" (Schroeder, (1998:75). Conversely, Adelman (1998) found that among top students in engineering, the four-year degree completion rates for men and women were similar. The debate centers, however, simply on whether male or female attrition is comparably higher. There is agreement that both men and women drop out of S&E, but because fewer women are in S&E to begin with, the impact may be larger for women.

A large set of variables underlies attrition from S&E (Seymour and Hewitt, 1997).[3] These variables affect both men and women, but they may affect women differently. Without oversimplifying, models of attrition tend to begin with attributes of the individual—that is, both the skills and goals that a student brings to college. Models end with an outcome or behavior: either persistence or the decision to leave. In the middle is a complex interaction of the individual with the institutional environment and external forces. Central points are the interactive nature of the relationship between the student and the institution (how a student fits into an institution), the role of multiple factors in predicting whether a student stays in S&E or not, and the longitudinal nature of the model—that is, students are constantly experiencing events, institutions are constantly making demands, and the decision-making process may be played out repeatedly over the course of a student's educational process (which is why some students may leave in their first term of college, while others leave just before graduating).[4]

---

[3]Seymour and Hewitt (1997) further note that the relative weights of these variables may differ across particular S&E disciplines—for example, between engineering and science and mathematics.

[4]Seymour and Hewitt (1997) note that switchers tend to give more reasons for switching than non-switchers give for staying—that is, students who switch out of S&E may do so for multiple reasons. An important consequence is that institutions may have to pursue multiple intervention strategies to keep students in S&E, although some students find that the solving of one large problem can convince them to persist.

At the universities visited, interviewees speculated about the causes of attrition of females. At one university interviewees noted some of the problems that could lead to the attrition of faculty or students, including a lack of female role models, young women's lack of knowledge about engineering, and the perception that "doing it all" is too hard. Similar views were voiced during other site visits. In fact, it was suggested that some younger women observe the long hours, stress, and lack of family time experienced by women academics and decide that "doing it all" is not for them.

> If you're a female, you have to prove yourself worthy to get invited into study groups and work on projects.
>
> —*Undergraduate student, during site visit*

What other factors account for the attrition of women students? Some researchers have pointed to the differences in male and female student demographics as an important factor in the probability of completion of an S&E degree. According to Peter and Horn (2005:v)

> While women have increased their representation among younger, full-time students, who tend to be more successful in completing a college degree, women continue to represent 60 percent or more of students with characteristics that place them at a disadvantage in succeeding in postsecondary education. In particular, women make up 60 percent of students in the lowest 25 percent income level, 62 percent of students age 40 or older, 62 percent of students with children or dependents (among married or separated students), and 69 percent of single parents. All of these characteristics are associated with lower rates of persistence and completion in postsecondary education (e.g., Berkner, He, and Cataldi 2002).

Another factor in the attrition of women students, as noted in Chapter 2, may be unequal student preparation. To reiterate: women are more likely to take such mathematics courses as geometry, algebra II, and trigonometry, whereas men are slightly more likely to take precalculus and calculus. Men may take more S&E prerequisite courses earlier than women. In addition, men are more likely to take physics and engineering, while women are more likely to take biology and chemistry (NSF, 2003: Appendix Table 1-1). Because mathematics is often viewed as a critical enabling course in science and engineering, it is important that women develop their mathematical skills prior to or early on in college. In fact, women may be at a relative disadvantage compared with men because of differences in mathematics preparation. Likewise, as noted in Chapter 2, female students interested in computer science sometimes have less experience than their male peers. The overall concern is simply that college is hard enough. Inadequate preparation, while it can certainly be made up during college, may put additional pressures on students, leaving them more inclined to leave a program of study. That said, studies that compared similarly qualified male and female students have found similar levels of persistence. These studies suggest that during the early college years women tend to lose some self-confidence, self-esteem, and ambitions for an S&E career, while men gain these attributes—that is, the problem is not moving from high school to college, but rather the difficulties experienced in the early years of college (Seymour and Hewitt, 1997).

Even more important perhaps are the negative experiences at college that may afflict women students more often or to a greater degree than male students (Seymour and Hewitt, 1997). One negative experience is harassment. Harassment, including sexual harassment, occurs on university campuses to students, faculty, and staff. It is more likely to be directed at women. Indeed, each year usually brings new media reports of harassment lawsuits involving universities and university personnel (Fogg, 2004; Wilson, 2004a). Yet some harassment may go unreported. Regardless of whether harassment is occurring on a campus, if several students or faculty members perceive it to be happening, then it is a challenge to women's retention and advancement.

That harassment had occurred on campus was intimated by interviewees during two of the site visits. At one university some faculty interviewees complained of sexual harassment, inappropriate comments about clothing, and patting on the head in the presence of undergraduates. At a second university some women students reported that they were harassed by male faculty. Yet all of the institutions selected for site visits had taken steps to be more female friendly.

Another experience that may cause women to rethink majoring in S&E is the isolation of female students. Isolation may occur for several reasons. The most obvious is that female students are underrepresented in many S&E courses. However, this is neither a necessary nor a sufficient cause. Rather, isolation occurs when students and faculty actions create such an outcome: male students may not want to work with female students; female students may assume male students do not want to work with them; faculty may segregate students.

Yet another factor that may lead to greater female attrition is students' expectations of the future—not only the remainder of their undergraduate schooling, but also their likelihood of entering graduate school, what they can expect from graduate school, and their career outlook. The concern is that female students will hear more negatives than male students, including that S&E is overwhelmingly male and that they will not do as well.

Lack of positive female role models may be held up as a factor underlying the attrition of female students. Of course, anyone can be a role model, but female students may view the absence of women faculty or the presence of unhappy female faculty as a sign that they are pursuing the wrong education.

A final challenge for the retention of female students is the undergraduate S&E curriculum, which scholars argue is much less interesting for those students. Indeed, this has been true for some time: "Historically, curricular content and teaching techniques in the sciences and engineering not only have done little to encourage girls and women to pursue their interests in these fields, but also have done damage, affecting girls and women negatively" (NSF, 1997). Busch-Vishniac and Jarosz (2004:258) describe how contemporary engineering curriculum may be less female friendly:

> The effects of a rigid segmentation of topics into courses with little communication among them are the isolation of most undergraduates from the engineering faculty until their 2nd or 3rd year, the presentation of a picture of engineering that is divorced from application until far into the curriculum, and distributed authority for the students that makes advising and mentoring difficult. We expect engineering students to be so committed to the engineering endeavor from the time they set foot on a campus that they will pursue courses that offer no insight into engineering as a profession for a minimum of a year, knowing that after this "hazing," there will be the reward of relevant classes. This sort of approach selectively disadvantages women and minorities, because they are less likely to be exposed to engineering as a profession and to be encouraged to pursue engineering careers. For these groups, the structure of our curriculum is downright unattractive, uninformative, and uninviting.

All this leads to negative attitudes that push for attrition rather than persistence.

Graduate Students

Losing graduate students from S&E programs is a particular concern, since they have presumably already invested much in S&E education. Evidence suggests that there might be gender differences in completion rates. Duke University found that in the biological sciences men were more likely to complete their doctorates than women (76 percent versus 67 percent). But, men and women had similar completion rates in the physical sciences and engineering (Siegel, 2005). There are various reasons why graduate students might drop out of S&E programs. In a survey of 3,300 students in chemistry, computer science, electrical engineering, and physics conducted in 1993-1994, Fox (2001) found that women were less likely than men to report being taken seriously and respected by faculty, being comfortable speaking in group meetings, and collaborating with male graduate students and faculty. In addition, it appeared that men received more help than women did in completing activities, such as writing grant proposals, coauthoring publications, and learning to design research. Finally, women were more likely than men to report that the relationship with their adviser was one of "student-and-faculty" compared with "mentor-mentee" or "colleagues." Such outcomes could increase the chances that female students might leave an S&E program.

Students leave a graduate program prior to completing a Ph.D. for various reasons that can be grouped into three categories: individual, institutional, and, perhaps the most important, the intersection of individual and institutional. Individual characteristics often relate to a student's prior preparation and expectations, compared with current expectations about the program and expectations about future career prospects. Self-confidence and self-esteem also may be issues. However, some scholars believe that the focus on the student is overemphasized, that institutional and organizational characteristics need further scrutiny, and that ultimately these characteristics may be more important explanatory factors in attrition (e.g., Golde, 1998; Lovitts, 2001).

Institutional factors include departmental funding, size of the graduate program, and the demographic characteristics of the faculty (Ferrer de Valero, 2001). For example, the departure of a faculty member—something students have no control over—may affect student retention and attrition. Departmental culture affects how comfortable students feel and is in part a function of the demographic makeup of faculty.

Interactive factors primarily revolve around the socialization of students. Socialization includes relationships with faculty, especially the adviser and mentor, but also relationships with peers. Women's persistence at or attrition from graduate S&E programs may differ from those of men because interactive factors operate differently for women than for men or because the factors are not equally important to both men and women. Ferreira (2003) notes that in graduate school women may find a chilly climate, may face harassment, and may not be engaged by faculty in professional socialization. If women graduate students are having more negative experiences in graduate school than those faced by men, they may be more inclined to leave.

BOX 3-1
Summary of Challenges

Female students may be more likely to leave undergraduate and graduate S&E programs for the following reasons:

✓ The demographic characteristics of females make them more at risk for attrition.
✓ Women may have negative experiences, including marginalization, isolation, or harassment.
✓ For female undergraduates, the curricula may not be as engaging as for male undergraduates.
✓ The characteristics of graduate programs, including departmental culture, may favor male students.
✓ Women may face financial issues.
✓ Women may more likely have negative, unsupportive, or missing relationships with advisors or mentors.

RETENTION STRATEGIES

Retaining Undergraduate Students

Many of the efforts to increase women's participation in science and engineering have focused on the entry point to academia, the undergraduate degree. The logic behind this emphasis is evident: a sufficient percentage of students must enter a university if a sufficient percentage is to move on into graduate studies and into academic employment. Although the transfer rate of undergraduates to the graduate path is likely to remain less than 100 percent, the argument is compelling that higher percentages at entry are necessary if higher percentages of students are to move to the more advanced levels.

BOX 3-2
Undergraduate Retention Strategies

✓ Have the institution signal the importance of women.
✓ Strengthen student advising.
✓ Establish mentoring programs.
✓ Change pedagogy.
✓ Increase engagement with students.
✓ Increase professional socialization.

There are other arguments as well for concentrating efforts on under-graduates. They are the largest cohort of students educated in academia, and the quality of the undergraduate student cohort is often the basis for judging quality among peer institutions. Moreover, accrediting require-ments, and the fact that undergraduate education is usually administered by a central office, allow changes to be widely implemented across an institution. Thus it is not surprising that many institutions have concen-trated on their undergraduate programs when considering initiatives to increase the participation of women.

Signaling the Importance of Women

At the institutional level, many different indicators can set the climate and signal that the institution as a whole is committed to advancing and retaining women. A relatively simple and low-cost step is to create and then exploit lines of communication between administrators and students. Simply communicating with female students that the institution values their presence can go a long way toward fighting the isolation and marginalization that female students might feel. Again, as noted in Chap-ter 2, any steps the institution can take to create a sense of inclusiveness—through outreach efforts by university officials and administrators di-rected toward students—would be welcome.

However, for an initiative to succeed in an academic setting, support must be forthcoming from all levels of the faculty and administration. Indeed, initiatives must proceed through a campus-accepted approval process and viewed as a priority at the highest levels. One example is the presidential-appointed diversity council described in Chapter 2. Univer-sities can create an office or appoint an official to deal with issues of concern to women. Indeed, many universities already have such offices or officials. Committees on the status of women, campus ombudsmen, and similar groups offer protections for students, places to which stu-dents can turn for help, advocacy mechanisms for female students, and entry points for providing further resources. It is imperative, however, that such groups advertise their presence clearly and widely. One group should be charged with monitoring student attrition, or, alternatively, such a task could be carried out by a senior official in the university's administration. For example, Carnegie Mellon University conducted hundreds of interviews with male and female students in computer sci-ence over a four-year period. Students were interviewed once per semes-ter. These data collected helped the university to identify obstacles to students' success (Blum, 2001).

Finally, on the policy side institutions can signal the value of female students by crafting female-friendly policies and generally improving the campus climate. Many such policies are in fact gender neutral, such as efforts to enhance campus security, which can certainly benefit any student. However, some policies and practices are specifically designed for female students, such as the creation of dedicated housing for female students in S&E (this initiative is described in more detail later in this chapter). Such a policy clearly indicates the willingness of the university to commit significant resources to supporting and advancing women students, and it acts as a mechanism for fighting isolation and marginalization. Another policy might be one of ensuring that "all students have a safe physical environment in which to work" (Cuny and Aspray, 2001:15). Yet another policy pursuit might be offering sexual harassment and diversity training to faculty, staff, and students.

The chancellor of one university made the improvement of campus "climate" a top priority. The central goals of the climate initiative were to create new opportunities for frank and open conversation and to determine how the climate issue is manifested on campus. According to the chancellor, a desirable climate adds ethnic and gender inclusiveness, as well as intellectual diversity. In fact, an improved climate benefits all students, faculty, and staff. Interviewees at one site visit mentioned that their university, in an attempt to improve the campus climate, undertook a comprehensive effort to make sexual harassment a university community concern. The effort was vigorously endorsed publicly by the administration and refined and renewed with an array of campus resources. Information sessions were offered to all employees; sexual harassment contact persons were identified and trained in every school, college, and division; and a cross-campus team of facilitators presented information sessions to the deans, administrative teams, academic departments, and support units.

Finally, as Cuny and Aspray (2001) note, universities and departments should publicize their successes in recruiting and retaining female students. Such visibility is no less important than the policies and practices undertaken to do so.

Strengthening Student Advising

Advising is a process that continues throughout a student's time of study at an institution. Advisers can both offer positive encouragement and serve as a frontline of defense for students experiencing problems (Lau, 2003). Cuny and Aspray (2001:15) suggest that universities "develop structural mechanisms that ensure that all students have good advising. Do not leave students at the mercy of a single, randomly assigned person. Have the department provide more than one advisor, perhaps a mentor or academic advisor in addition to a thesis advisor. Have the faculty review each student's progress every year. Have the students confidentially review their advisors each year. Make it easy for students to switch advisors." Seymour and Hewitt (1997:30) note that one of the distinguishing characteristics of "survivors"—those who stayed in S&E in college—was serendipity: "Serendipity . . . played a part in persistence, often in the form of intervention by faculty at a critical point in the student's academic or personal life." One way to increase the chances of this happening is through continual advising and mentoring.

Establishing Mentoring Programs

Women role models can have a significant influence on women students, particularly as they move into upper-level courses and begin thinking about career choices.[5] Visible female leadership can serve as an example of how an academic career choice can work for women. At the graduate student and faculty levels, role models can provide students with guideposts for navigating their way down a scientific career path. If such role models are not available on campus, or the field of study sends a majority of its graduates into nonacademic employment sectors (such as industry or government), the university can bring women role models to campus to give insights into careers outside academia. Another alternative may be the use of web-based mentoring to increase students' access to female science professionals "even if they are geographically dispersed and inaccessible locally" (Packard, 2003:54). However, where both options are available, face-to-face mentoring and advising may be preferable to "distance mentoring."

Mentoring plays a significant role in whether students advance in science and engineering. For students who may be the first in their families to attend college, mentoring may lead to the pursuit of graduate study. However, successful mentoring is a challenge. An important element is the need to separate mentoring from oversight. For undergraduates, the authority of the faculty member who may have decision-making power over grades may be too intimidating a factor in a mentoring relationship.

Mentoring should not be equated with formal advising, which most campuses have in some form. In undergraduate advising, faculty are as-

---

[5]Mentors of either gender, though, can be effective (Whitten et al., 2003). Good advice for mentors can be found in Chapter 5, "Mentoring and Being Mentored," of *Making the Right Moves: A Practical Guide to Scientific Management for Post Doctoral and New Faculty* by the Burroughs Wellcome Fund and the Howard Hughes Medical Institute, 2004, available at http://www.hhmi.org/grants/pdf/labmgmt/book.pdf. Accessed April 20, 2005.

signed to advise students on making course choices (and changes) and dealing with degree program requirements. Mentoring is an approach that aims to guide students to a successful transition from one stage of their academic advancement to the next. Mentoring may include engaging undergraduate students in research and guiding them along a research path, such as attending and presenting a paper at a conference, exploring scholarship or fellowship opportunities, and encouraging applications to graduate school (COSEPUP, 1997).

Many students look to other students for support and mentoring. Undergraduate students at the universities visited relied on students a year or two ahead to give advice about ways to navigate the degree program, difficult courses, internships, and so forth. Less often did undergraduates turn to graduate students, because frequently they were teaching assistants with authority over course grades. On some campuses, a women students' group might organize a talk by a graduate of the university so that she can share her views on career opportunities and what is needed to get good jobs. Upper division students, especially, found that such an event produced extremely useful and practical information, because it addressed the issue they were all facing: employment after graduation.

At one university, although the female population was increasing to a critical mass, a faculty member was hired to invigorate mentoring efforts for both undergraduate and graduate women. Because previous efforts to form a self-sustaining women's support group had not caught on, the university's president made a financial commitment to fund the faculty member's support organization, which focused on women in computer science, and her full-time work on mentoring women. With dedicated annual funding from the president, the support organization carried out these activities:

• organized social events aimed at increasing the participation of female students by providing them with an opportunity to network, form friendships, and plan collaborations;

• supported an advice network, speakers' program, alumnae links, biweekly lunches, student-faculty dinners, group outings, career forums, and other social and academic events;

• ran a big sister/little sister program for undergraduates, pairing upper division and graduate students with first-year and sophomore computer science majors;

• actively encouraged undergraduate women to find faculty research projects and mentors; and

• participated in the annual celebration of women in computing.

A provost contrasted this list of activities with the lack of women's programs elsewhere: "In most other departments and schools there is nothing for women."

The guide *Adviser, Teacher, Role Model, Friend: On Being a Mentor to Students in Science and Engineering* prepared by the National Academies suggests that faculty members mentoring undergraduates concentrate on building a respectful mentoring relationship and responding to various student issues (COSEPUP, 1997). To build trust, this guide suggests that faculty

- take students seriously,
- do not dictate answers,
- be frank and direct,
- help students to develop self-esteem,
- invite other mentors,
- address fears without belittling, and
- meet on "neutral ground."

Mentors should help students with, among other things, early fears and concerns (especially for those students who are the first in their family to attend college) about ability and preparation; coursework and academic goals; undergraduate research experience; and whether or not to pursue graduate study.

Making Pedagogical Changes

The argument for changing the content or the way S&E is taught to promote diversity rests on the assumption that men and women learn differently or appreciate content differently. Hypothetically, it could be said that female students do not fare as well in courses in which the manner of instruction relies heavily on group projects and group study, because female students tend to find themselves on the outside of such groups.[6] Or, female students fare less well in S&E courses that fail to connect the material taught to real-world applications. Farrell (2002:31) points out that the "conventional wisdom holds that women are more inclined to study subjects they find socially relevant." Studies back up this wisdom (e.g., Busch-Vishniac and Jarosz, 2004). Universities may find that, steps to make curricula more applied and more relevant result in greater interest from women in that curricula.

---

[6]Alternatively, female students may do better in team-oriented courses, assuming they are included, than in other types of courses.

Finally, because technology is playing a larger role in the classroom and being applied in novel ways to deliver course content to the students, it is important to ask whether men and women benefit differently from such changes. At one university visited, the faculty considered making changes to both content and instruction:

> We need to do a better job [of introducing freshmen to interesting material]. Our intro is pretty hard core: programming, data structures. More applied courses come in junior and senior years, but that's a long time to wait.
>
> —*Department chair, during a site visit*

• A course in discrete mathematics, a subject foreign to most new women students, was expanded to include more motivational examples and "grand challenge" problems to illustrate the relevance of the subject. This approach is believed to appeal to women students and to teach "computing with a purpose."

• A faculty member who teaches the first required course in serious programming said she and her colleagues were introducing interesting applications, such as game planning, and bringing more guest speakers to talk about applications.

It is also important to note that efforts to change pedagogy and course content can diminish student learning outcomes. For example, Busch-Vishniac and Jarosz (2004:256) found that "most diversity initiatives aimed at the undergraduate engineering student population have started with a curriculum that is known to be unattractive to women and minorities and have tried using 'add-ons' or minor changes to rectify the situation." They argue that this approach fails because the add-ons simply place more pressure on the students, but do not fundamentally fix the problems in the curriculum.

In view of this problem, it is still not entirely clear what changes would be beneficial. Some of the obvious changes that could help to retain any student including women are offering supplemental instruction (e.g., tutoring services) and having faculty endorse and encourage the use of student support services (Amenkhienan and Kogan, 2004).

Increasing Engagement with Female Students

Retaining women students, particularly in the physical sciences and engineering, has proved to be an ongoing challenge for many institutions. One of the critical points is the second year of the degree program when any student prone to transfer often does so. Of the many possible reasons for attrition, some reasons identified by women are a sense of isolation, because there are so few other women in their area of study, and difficulty in finding a study or project group. Some institutions have established programs that specifically address this weak point. The first policy response by institutions is to find a mechanism for bringing female students together. Such a step can create a more supportive environment and make it easier for female students to access resources and for faculty support to reach the students. Site visits to successful physics departments have suggested that identifying and engaging potential majors early on is critical in retaining students (Whitten et al., 2003).

In many undergraduate programs women are a very small fraction of the enrollment. The programs at one institution were targeted toward building a community of women so that women students did not feel isolated. A teaching assistant, widely recognized to be the best, was assigned to the women in the engineering section. Some male students expressed resentment, however, at the perceived special treatment for women, wondering why there were no "men in engineering" programs. A woman student replied, "There is; it's called [name of institution]."

One university created a "women in science and engineering" program in response to the disproportionate loss of women from science majors during the first two years and to women's feelings of isolation. Several years later the program was housing over 100 female freshmen and sophomore science and engineering majors in their own residence hall. Women in the program take important foundation courses together and have special lab and discussion sections, access to lab instructors at regular office hours in their dorm, and a nearby study partner. They are able to know one another, meet women working in diverse technical fields, attend special study sections, explore career possibilities, and attend special cultural events. According to faculty advisers, students in the program earn higher science grades than students in the program who do not attend the special study sections and students outside the program overall. According to the anecdotal evidence, most of those who join tend to stay in the program and build relationships with other students.

Special housing for women in science and engineering exists in several colleges and universities. The first residence hall for women in S&E was established in 1989 by Douglass College at Rutgers, the State University of New Jersey.[7] Since that time, universities such as the University of California, Berkeley, University of Wisconsin, Purdue University, and University of Michigan have dedicated space for women in science and engineering. By locating women together in a shared space, it becomes

---

[7]See Douglass College: The Douglass Project, at http://www.rci.rutgers.edu/~dougproj/. Accessed February 27, 2006.

easier for the university to offer events and programs that engage female students, such as lectures, dinners, and tutoring sessions (Black, 1999). For example, the University of Arizona created a living-learning environment for women in science, engineering, math, and technology that offers programs and services such as mentoring, tutoring, study groups, writing assistance, and social and cultural events.[8]

A complementary approach to such university-led programs is a bottom-up approach, such as female S&E students joining a professional society (which could, of course, also be started by interested faculty and staff). For example, in 1999 female engineering and computer science students at Baylor University organized a student section of the Society of Women Engineers (SWE). In an assessment of the benefits of this organization, Fry and Allgood (2002) found support for the hypothesis that SWE membership was associated with increased retention of female students. Dozens of universities have Women in Engineering (WIE) or Women in Science and Engineering (WISE) programs. These programs undertake a large variety of activities, including recruitment and outreach, scholarships, mentoring, career development and exploration, study skills, social opportunities, support, and publicity (Knight and Cunningham, 2004). Research—although still being developed, refined, and implemented— has suggested that these programs are beneficial (Marra and Bogue, 2004).

Whitten et al. (2003) have suggested additional steps faculty can take to "encourage the growth of a warm and inclusive student culture":

- a student lounge
- a tutorial service
- lab assistants
- seminars
- a chapter of a professional society or club
- social activities

Increasing Professional Socialization

Universities can help to foster a sense of "being a scientist or engineer" among students in three ways: (1) through research experience, (2) through presentations, and (3) through participation in mentoring, tutoring, or recruitment efforts. The research exposure of undergraduates in S&E could be quite flexible lasting for weeks, a semester, a year, or longer. As Gonzalez (2001:1624) notes, undergraduate research is already a com-

---

[8]See University of Arizona, Residence Life, Campus Housing, WISE, at http://www.life. arizona.edu/prospectiveresidents/wise.asp. Accessed April 6, 2005.

mon occurrence on campus: "Faculty members are integrating undergraduate students into the research enterprise in a more deliberate fashion than ever before. Undergraduate research programs are proliferating, and undergraduate research conferences and journals are becoming a permanent fixture on the university's landscape." Most important, undergraduate research is beneficial to the students who participate, to faculty, and to the institution (Lopatto, 2005).

Under the heading "How Can Undergraduates Be Involved in Faculty Research?" Lancy (2003:91) raises some instructive questions:

- Are undergraduates involved in the faculty member's research? Is the work treated as an apprenticeship, with tasks graded in level of responsibility?
- Are graduate and undergraduate students brought together in a collaborative atmosphere where the entire research enterprise is the guided discussion? Is the undergraduate given increasingly complex tasks beyond washing test tubes?
- In writing grants, are undergraduate research assistants written into the budget? In writing National Science Foundation grants, is a Research Experiences for Undergraduates supplement requested (available at http://www.nsf.gov/search97cgi/vtopic/)?
- Is the faculty member aware of and does he or she take advantage of any campus programs that provide funds to support undergraduate research?
- Do students participate in data analysis, write-up, presentation, and publication?
- Do undergraduates travel to conferences with the faculty mentor? Are they socialized into the profession or discipline?
- Are students involved in consulting done by the faculty member?

As for the second aspect of professional socialization, presenting student research, Kinkead (2003) suggests that undergraduate research be "celebrated." This can be done on campus, at university-hosted conferences, at professional society meetings, and in publications. Some colleges and universities host student conferences. A very competitive example is the University of California (UC)'s effort to showcase undergraduate student research as part of its UC Day. A competition is held to select two outstanding abstracts describing research projects from each of the eight undergraduate UC campuses.[9]

---

[9]For more information, see University of California—UC Research Opportunities for Undergraduates at http://www.universityofcalifornia.edu/research/undergrad.html. Accessed April 6, 2005.

Finally, students could take an active role in recruiting new undergraduates. An event tends to be successful when students (undergraduate and graduate) help to plan the event; when students serve as demonstrators in projects; when the demonstration projects used have real-world applications; and when some capacity is provided for a hands-on interaction. An additional component is industry participation. Corporations are generally looking for the recruits who can best contribute to their organization. An early acquaintance with a company, especially if it offers an internship or co-op program with the department, often produces the best recruits for the company.

Retaining Graduate Students

As noted in Chapter 2, the department plays a particularly significant role in the lives of graduate students. The faculty, especially the thesis adviser, has a large impact on the retention of women graduate students. "A student's relationship with his or her adviser is probably the single most critical factor in determining who stays and who leaves" (Lovitts, 2001:270). The thesis adviser can ensure that women graduate students are included in meetings and seminars, as well as social activities centered on the research group. The adviser can be watchful of practices that marginalize women students and their contributions. Women graduate students should be afforded at least the same resources afforded male graduate students.

BOX 3-3
Graduate Student Retention Strategies

✓ Have the institution signal the importance of women.
✓ Improve advising and mentoring.
✓ Increase engagement with students.
✓ Increase professional socialization.
✓ Make funding more secure.
✓ Provide students with constructive feedback.

Signaling the Importance of Women

Institutions can indicate support of graduate students in general and of women in a number of ways. As discussed in Chapter 2, institutions provide infrastructure such as housing and health insurance.

The department chair can lead the effort to offer the motivational signaling of support for women graduate students. The chair can reinforce institutional policy on sexual harassment and initiate and institutionalize departmental policies that facilitate retention.

Cuny and Aspray (2001) suggest that institutions broaden the culture of their departments—in traditional, male-oriented departments, women may feel less at home— and that departments seek to be transparent in their policies, so students do not have to be part of an informal social network to learn about such matters.

Lovitts (2001:265) prescribes self-assessment: "To address the problem of attrition, universities and departments—especially ones with high student and faculty attrition rates—need to assess their cultures and their climates." She goes on to point out that "universities can best learn about the underlying causes of attrition by opening up channels of communication with current and exiting graduate students. In particular, universities can better learn about students' concerns and discontents by sponsoring focus group discussions with currently enrolled graduate students on an ongoing basis."

Improving Mentoring

"Mentoring may be the most important variable related to academic and career success for graduate students" (Boyle and Boice, 1998:90). Most thesis advisers also serve as mentors for their graduate students, guiding them through graduate school and pointing out the career paths that lie beyond. Ideally, this is a mutually beneficial arrangement, but the supervisory role that thesis advisers play can also inject some conflict into the mentor-mentee relationship. Mentoring has already been examined at length by the National Academies (COSEPUP, 1997). In that report, the authors note several ways in which mentors may be able to assist graduate students:

- helping students choose a graduate school
- helping students choose an adviser
- helping students select an appropriate degree program
- planning an appropriate curriculum
- choosing a thesis committee
- helping students adjust to graduate school (e.g., teaching them organizational or time management skills)
- assisting in a student's professional growth

The Committee on Graduate Education of the Association of American Universities (1998) noted that "faculty mentors should confer with students frequently to assess students' progress, and should provide the department with periodic assessments on progress to the degree." Moreover, "institutions and departments should clearly affirm the importance of faculty mentoring through policy guidelines and incentives." Departments can facilitate mentoring and advising by establishing programs in which students can socialize with all the faculty and advanced graduate students (Boyle and Boice, 1998). Mentoring should be a valued part of a faculty member's activities, for which faculty could be rewarded.

> Within [a few] years of when I arrived, they hired seven women; we're now a third of the department. This critical mass is essential. Graduate students say this is the best thing about our department—having all these different role models.
>
> —*Faculty member,*
> *during site visit*

Increasing Professional Socialization

Much like undergraduates, but more so, female graduate students need to experience and enjoy professional socialization. First, new graduate students should be socialized into the expectations of graduate education, including theses, examinations, and dissertations, but in a collegial way involving faculty and advanced graduate students (Lovitts, 2001). Second, all graduate students could be exposed to the research experience. Universities could, for example, monitor students receiving research assistantships and teaching assistantships to ensure women are not disproportionately receiving the latter. Universities also could monitor instances in which graduate students are able to place their names on scientific papers that incorporate research to which they contributed. Indeed, research productivity is often measured in terms of citations, and it is important for women to work on research projects and share in efforts to present findings at conferences or in publication. Finally, all students could be encouraged to join professional associations and societies, to attend their meetings, and to present papers or posters.

Efforts to foster collegiality may benefit from placing students in communal offices (Boyle and Boice, 1998). Collegiality is needed as well between graduate classes, not just within one class of students. Advanced students can serve as informal advisers to more junior students.

Providing Secure Funding for Graduate Students

The time that is required to complete a Ph.D. degree in science and technology seems to be growing. Thus insufficient funding may contribute to attrition. Departments need to find ways to guarantee funding for the duration of a graduate student's enrollment (within reasonable limits). "Gender differences are small in certain indicators of financial support for graduate training" (Fox, 2001:657), but these measures are often quantitative and do not measure qualitative issues. Departments could assess what types of funding graduate students receive and what student outcomes are linked to different types of funding.

Providing Constructive Feedback

Graduate students are more likely to complete their requirements faster within a programmatic framework that includes and fosters timely feedback and greater structure (Boyle and Boice, 1998). Departments could provide greater structure for students by establishing more regular meetings and setting some deadlines for students, such as to find an adviser. Finally, department faculty can endeavor to offer quick feedback on a student's progress.

Retaining Postdoctoral Fellows

A recent report by the Committee on Science, Engineering, and Public Policy at the National Academies (COSEPUP, 2000:99) recommended 10 steps that advisers, institutions, funding organizations, and disciplinary societies could take to aid postdoctoral fellows:

1. Award institutional recognition, status, and compensation commensurate with the postdocs' contributions to the research enterprise.

2. Develop distinct policies and standards for postdocs, modeled on those available for graduate students and faculty.

3. Develop mechanisms for frequent and regular communication between postdocs and their advisers, institutions, funding organizations, and disciplinary societies.

4. Monitor and provide formal evaluations (at least annually) of the performance of postdocs.

5. Ensure that all postdocs have access to health insurance, regardless of funding source, and to institutional services.

6. Set limits for total time as a postdoc (of approximately five years, summing time at all institutions), with clearly described exceptions as appropriate.

7. Invite the participation of postdocs when creating standards, definitions, and conditions for appointments.

8. Provide substantive career guidance to improve postdocs' ability to prepare for regular employment.

9. Improve the quality of data both for postdoctoral working conditions and for the population of postdocs in relation to employment prospects in research.

10. Take steps to improve the transition of postdocs to regular career positions.

CONCLUSION

Enrolling women students in science and technology degree programs is not enough; universities must do what is possible, within the context of limited resources, to retain them through the rigors of an S&E degree program, the challenges of a thesis project, and the search for a research or academic career. Institutions must continually remind students that there are promising careers in S&E, but doing so requires better communications among institutions, departments, and faculty, on the one hand, and students, on the other. A consistent message of support, backed up by a commitment from faculty, can go a long way to supporting students during their journey.

BOX 3-4
Summary of Strategies for Retaining Women Undergraduate,
Graduate, and Postdoctoral Students

What faculty can do:

- Advise and mentor prospective and current female undergraduate, graduate, and postdoctoral students.
- Conduct outreach to K-12 institutions to help prepare women for college and to combat negative attitudes about the place of women in science and engineering.
- Advise and encourage female students in science and engineering groups.
- Invite female students to participate in research opportunities.
- Participate in bridge programs, campus visits, lectures, and seminars.
- Encourage female students to give presentations at conferences.
- Make curricula more practically relevant and ask whether all students are equally aided by different instructional techniques and technologies.

What department chairs can do:

- Create an image of the department as female friendly and feature this image in promotional materials and on the department's web site.
- Communicate with faculty about the importance of diversity in recruiting.
- Support and reinforce a faculty member's commitment to advising and encouraging female students and postdocs through service awards and recognition during tenure and promotion reviews.
- Monitor the allocation of resources to students and survey students' opinions.
- Meet with faculty to assess the relationship of curricular content and instruction methods to student learning outcomes for male and female students.

What deans and provosts can do:

- Devote resources to female undergraduate students—mentoring, advising, tutoring services, and if feasible, separate housing.
- Craft female-friendly policies on campus.
- Monitor departments' progress in increasing the percentage of female students and postdocs.
- Conduct school-wide assessments of status of women.

What presidents can do:

- Publicly state the institution's commitment to diversity and inclusiveness whenever possible.
- Create an institutional structure, such as a standing committee, to address diversity issues within the student body. Charge that committee with monitoring diversity across the institution and with making recommendations to increase diversity.
- Demonstrate the institution's commitment by meeting with female students and postdocs and devoting resources to programs that assist them.

4

Recruiting Women Faculty

At most universities and colleges a doctorate is the minimum threshold to enter a career in academia. Fortunately, those recruiting faculty are seeing the number of women receiving Ph.D.'s in science and engineering (S&E) increasing (Figure 4-1).

The figure reveals that by 2001 "females earned 37 percent of S&E and 57 percent of non-S&E doctoral degrees, up from 8 and 18 percent, respectively, in 1966" (NSF, 2004c). By field, women received from about 10 percent (mechanical engineering) to 67 percent (psychology) of the doctorate degrees awarded in 2001 (Table 4-1).

A fair amount of these female Ph.D.'s would be expected to choose academia for their careers. After all, statistics show that women prefer to work in academia, compared with industry or government employment. Yet the percentages of women actually in academic jobs suggest that preference does not predict outcome. Proportionately more women are employed in academia at two-year and four-year institutions; proportionately fewer are employed at top research institutions (NRC, 2001). A recent study of female faculty examined the percentage of male and female tenured and tenure-track faculty in several disciplines, including S&E, at the top 50 U.S. educational institutions, based on research expenditures (Nelson and Rogers, 2004). The percentage of assistant professors who were women and the percentage of doctorates received by women were contrasted with similar percentages for men. The study found that a larger percentage of Ph.D.'s went to women, while a smaller percentage of assis-

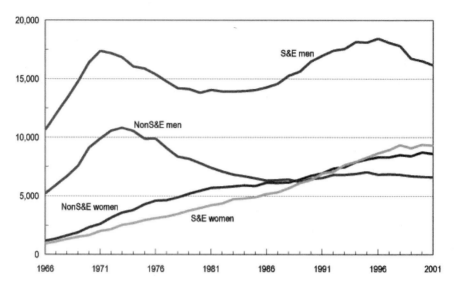

FIGURE 4-1 Doctoral degrees received, by broad field and gender, 1966-2001.
SOURCE: NSF (2004c).

tant professor positions were held by women; whereas the trend is the opposite for men (Table 4-2).

This chapter explores the challenges and strategies for recruiting women into tenure-track, assistant professor positions—a traditional starting point for the academic career. Almost always, associate or full professors have risen to their positions from that of assistant professor. Although non-tenure-track jobs, such as lecturer or instructor positions and adjunct positions, are available, these positions do not offer the same prestige or security potential as tenure-track positions.

CHALLENGES

Two basic challenges confront university and college officials seeking to recruit additional female faculty. First, the perception is that women prefer certain types of institutions for employment. Second, women also perceive that they have less of a chance of being hired than male candidates do, all other things being equal.

Research suggests that female science faculty are more likely to be employed by community colleges or institutions that do not offer a doctoral degree than by large research universities (Schneider, 2000). Thus "at the country's big research universities, the vast majority of professors are men" (Wilson, 2004b). A 2002 analysis found that 71 percent of full-time female mathematics faculty were employed at institutions that offer no higher than a master's or bachelor's degree. To take one example, women in mathematics make up 29 percent and 31 percent, respectively, of the full-time faculty at master's- and baccalaureate-granting institutions, but only about 12 percent of the full-time faculty at the most prestigious research universities (Kirkman et al., 2003).

> It's hard to persuade female graduates that an academic career would be a good thing. We need to be concerned about the pipeline, or we won't have enough future faculty.
>
> —*Dean, during site visit*

Why would women prefer to go into another employment sector or into research institutions that do not grant doctorates? Perceptions of working conditions at the major research universities, which are perceived to be more negative for women than for men, may be one reason.

An associate dean for sciences at one of the research universities visited described presenting a workshop on how to apply for academic positions. When he asked women students how many were interested in such positions, only about 10 percent raised their hands. They cited negative perceptions of the tenure clock and the six to seven years of graduate work required as reasons. The dean commented: "We're competing with liberal arts colleges and industry, especially for chemistry, where they find better working conditions."

Working conditions can be framed in two ways: policies and practices and departmental or institutional culture. Women may find less support or less of a welcome in both respects.

One way in which the academic environment may be less welcoming to women occurs when the departmental or institutional culture is more supportive of male academics. A male department chair at one university noted that although the majority of departments favor the advancement of women, "bad stories have to do with the particular culture in certain units." He expressed frustration that some departments seemed unable to remove such "cultural baggage." Interviewees at another university noted lingering male resistance and occasional harassment by male faculty. Interviewees at a third university posited that a minority of male engineers resist the inclusion of women not only in certain other cultures, but also in the United States, where women do not fit the engineering image for some traditional faculty.

Hostile cultures can result in a lack of action to support change, overt action to undermine or prevent change, or discriminatory action. At one institution that had created a faculty mentoring program, some people

TABLE 4-1 S&E Doctoral Degrees Awarded to Women, by Field, 1994-2001

Field	Number			
	1994	1995	1996	1997
All S&E fields	7,921	8,287	8,651	8,936
Sciences	7,286	7,591	7,874	8,186
Agricultural sciences	249	228	282	260
Biological sciences	2,109	2,217	2,415	2,495
Computer sciences	137	186	139	150
Earth, atmospheric, and ocean sciences	183	170	172	209
Atmospheric	26	23	22	25
Earth	95	91	88	119
Oceanography	38	28	39	38
Other	24	28	23	27
Mathematics and statistics	236	265	231	263
Physical sciences	828	878	842	852
Astronomy	25	30	41	37
Chemistry	625	661	605	613
Physics	175	182	193	193
Other	3	5	3	9
Psychology	2,101	2,181	2,331	2,365
Social sciences	1,443	1,466	1,462	1,592
Anthropology	225	237	225	261
Area and ethnic studies	65	65	76	52
Economics	249	279	263	266
History of science	10	17	10	13
Linguistics	134	102	113	135
Political science and public administration	282	266	305	298
Sociology	283	294	276	334
Other	195	206	194	233
Engineering	635	696	777	750
Aerospace	11	14	24	16
Chemical	113	109	143	122
Civil	80	76	79	80
Electrical	147	173	169	150
Mechanical	69	64	78	88
Materials	83	95	84	106
Industrial	33	50	51	40
Other	99	115	149	148

SOURCE: NSF (2004c).

even worried that the mentors might be sued by the mentees who failed to get tenure.

A lack of diversity in the department and among majors also may deter some women from applying for faculty positions. According to interviewees at another university, for both potential faculty and students

				Percent	
1998	1999	2000	2001	1994	2001
9,347	9,086	9,384	9,303	30.2	36.5
8,573	8,297	8,547	8,378	35.7	41.9
298	280	274	288	23.1	34.0
2,536	2,394	2,618	2,545	40.5	44.8
159	156	141	155	15.2	18.8
219	210	230	236	22.2	31.5
30	22	33	28	20.2	24.1
127	112	109	115	18.7	29.2
32	45	46	45	30.4	37.8
30	31	42	48	39.3	40.0
297	277	258	276	21.1	27.4
926	831	835	834	20.8	24.6
45	33	40	41	17.4	22.0
695	632	624	628	27.7	31.7
177	160	163	155	11.3	13.0
9	6	8	10	10.7	32.3
2,455	2,453	2,410	2,296	62.2	66.9
1,683	1,696	1,781	1,748	37.0	42.9
262	275	276	262	53.8	58.5
63	59	67	95	53.3	66.0
312	291	293	306	22.6	28.2
19	18	17	8	37.0	20.0
123	148	134	136	60.6	59.4
364	356	365	328	30.3	33.4
317	342	374	337	51.6	58.4
223	207	255	276	36.5	48.1
774	789	837	925	10.9	16.8
15	17	21	28	4.8	13.8
140	123	151	180	15.6	24.8
100	89	88	111	11.7	18.7
156	155	195	203	8.8	12.9
93	96	96	91	6.8	9.5
84	88	83	105	15.4	21.0
40	43	35	44	14.5	21.5
146	178	168	163	13.6	21.8

the lack of a diverse faculty serves as a deterrent to recruitment and to a rewarding employment experience. A department with a healthy ratio of female faculty members may find it has reduced the risks of marginalization or isolation of any single faculty member and quelled the concerns of a prospective female hire who may be concerned about how

TABLE 4-2 Male and Female Tenure-Track Faculty at Top 50 U.S. Educational Institutions (percent)

Discipline	Female		Male	
	Assistant Professors (%)	Ph.D. Attainment (%) (1993–2002)	Assistant Professors (%)	Ph.D. Attainment (%) (1993–2002)
Biological sciences	30.2	44.7	69.8	55.2
Chemistry (FY 2003)	21.5	31.3	78.5	68.6
Math	19.6	27.2	80.5	72.7
Computer science	10.8	20.5	89.2	79.2
Astronomy (FY 2004)	22.0	20.6	78.0	79.0
Physics	11.2	13.3	88.8	86.6
Chemical engineering	21.4	22.3	78.7	77.2
Civil engineering	22.3	18.7	77.8	81.3
Electrical engineering	10.9	11.5	89.2	88.5
Mechanical engineering	15.7	10.4	84.4	89.6
Economics	19.0	29.3	81.0	70.5
Political science	36.5	36.6	63.5	63.0
Sociology	52.3	58.9	47.7	41.0
Psychology	45.4	66.1	54.6	33.9

NOTE: Percentages may not sum to 100 due to rounding.
SOURCE: Adapted from Nelson and Rogers (2004).

women in a department with no or only one other current female faculty member are treated.

A second challenge in recruiting women is that even when they do apply, they are not selected for the position. One reason is that search committees do not cast a wide enough net. One specific issue raised during the site visits was that a thorough search that tries to include women and minorities is more difficult and time consuming than older hiring practices that presumably expended less effort to increase the percentage of women in the applicant pool. Because "casting the net really wide" and then securing the approval of the dean and provost take so much time, the "best" candidates are often gone before an offer can be made. Acknowledgment of this situation is not to suggest that efforts should not be made to identify female and minority candidates. Rather, it suggests that such candidates are not currently plugged into the hiring network and that it takes a long time to find them.

Search committees may evaluate women harder than men. In fact, there is some evidence that both men and women evaluate women harder than men, and one study even found that both men and women preferred male candidates (Steinpreis et al., 1999).

> We need to convince a lot of people here that we need diversity, and that diversity vs. quality is a false tradeoff.
>
> —*University president, during site visit*

In Why So Slow (2004), a study of the advancement of women in academia, Valian posits a gender schema, a mental framework or construct that conceptualizes a person or group, can influence the way that men and women are evaluated. Women have to work much harder to be evaluated as highly as men—that is, women are undervalued, often in little ways that build up over time to significant disadvantage (Valian, 1998, 2004). One consequence of faculty holding these schemas is that hiring decisions are subtly pushed toward favoring male candidates. If Valian's argument is correct, then some search committees may not be aware they are acting in a biased fashion. One survey asked a group of search committee chairs responsible for searches in psychology departments how important 30 factors were in the job search and departmental decision process. The results revealed that the applicant's gender had a mean score of 1.38, with 1 equal to "not at all important" and 2 equal to "slightly important" on a four-point scale (Landrum and Clump, 2004).

BOX 4-1
Summary of Challenges

✓ Academe is one of several career choices for both men and women. Women, however, may find major research universities less attractive than other academic institutions and may be less inclined to seek employment in this sector.

• Perceptions of working conditions are more negative for women than for men.

• A lack of diversity in the department and among majors may deter some women from applying.

✓ Women with similar qualifications have less probability of being hired than male candidates.

• Search committees do not cast a wide net.

• Search committees evaluate women more rigidly than men.

STRATEGIES

In hiring female faculty, two general issues arise: how to get more women to apply and how to increase the percentage of women selected. Universities have directed much of their attention toward the first issue. However, both challenges can be addressed by motivated universities.

A professor at one university said that the department as a whole must be enthusiastic about new hires. The best solution is the most difficult: raising the consciousness of search committees and persuading them to work the phones and keep looking—even when qualified candidates are already apparent—in order to include women in the short list of candidates to be interviewed.

As noted earlier, at the universities visited, the percentage of women faculty recruited has increased, indicating the success of the programs and changes that these institutions have put into place. Most of the programs involved efforts to increase the percentage of women in applicant pools or to improve the climate for women faculty on campus. Many of these programs, such as child care, potentially benefit all faculty.

BOX 4-2
Strategies for Recruiting Women Faculty

✓ Have the institution signal the importance of female faculty by making positive declarative statements, establishing a committee on women, exercising oversight over the hiring process, and devoting resources to hiring women.

✓ Modify and expand faculty recruiting programs by creating special faculty lines, diversifying search committees, encouraging intervention by deans, and assessing past hiring efforts.

✓ Improve institutional policies and practices such as the tenure clock, child care, leave, spousal hiring, and training to combat harassment.

✓ Improve the success rate of women candidates by means of career advising, networking, and enhancing qualifications.

Signaling the Importance of Female Faculty

At the institutions visited, top administrators very publicly supported the goal of advancing women and acted on those statements. Interviewees at one university felt that the dean and provost were critical to building women faculty participation from the top, because they can influence new hiring and provide funding. General approaches are implemented by an institution, but often the committee found that the impetus for the change originated with an individual, usually an individual with the power at the institution to lead, set, and enforce policy. For example, interviewees attributed recent progress at one university to many different forces and individuals over two decades, but also to the fact that the current provost had professed his determination to hire more women. The levels of power varied; some were deans, some were provosts, some were department chairs. At each level, actions were taken that spurred changes. The actions taken, and the policies set and adhered to, conveyed the message that these initiatives, programs, and efforts were not cosmetic, but represented commitment by the individuals and the institutions to bringing about change.

It was noted, however, that such "inspired" individuals were present on all of these campuses; they were not unique. Such an individual was seen as an insider, one who really understood the institution, but who may have absorbed the concepts and ideas elsewhere or outside the institution. For example, at one institution a sabbatical spent at a federal agency led one dean to institute the new policies he had encountered elsewhere.

Institutional signaling also can be carried out by adding a diversity component to an institution's strategic plan either at the level of the institution or, in the case of one school visited, at the college or school level. By incorporating the women's advancement initiative into its strategic plan, this institution ensured that the goals would be institutionalized into the infrastructure of the university. As suggested by the college of engineering's strategic plan, various areas could be profitably addressed in such a document—that is, it could include statements on improving the climate by making it fairer or more equitable; crafting a clear and transparent hiring policy, one that also promotes the idea of inclusiveness; or making administrative officials responsible for departmental progress in diversifying faculty.

Yet another form of institutional signaling is to create an organizational mechanism for oversight into departmental hiring practices. At a minimum, deans and provosts can remind faculty search committees that one component of the search is a diversity element. The engineering department at one university recognized that search committees are not usually trained for their jobs. It therefore put together a training program and "faculty hiring toolkit." The dean had input into the process, requiring that each search list include women and minorities. Today, each search committee must be approved by the dean and provost. During the reporting process, the dean's office ensures that, even if the committee does not recommend a woman or minority candidate, it did cast its net widely. The dean receives the curriculum vitae of all finalists, including those not hired, and the dean and provost either approve the process or order the search extended.

> It's important for everyone to know they're not lowering the bar in hiring women.
>
> —*Faculty member,*
> *during site visit*

Another signal is to create a committee on the status of women or assign a powerful administrator oversight on the issue of diversity at the institution. Some institutions appointed dedicated senior administrative personnel to address faculty diversity, such as a vice provost or dean. Others placed women on advisory boards and university committees that wielded significant power on the campus. A similar step was taken recently at Princeton, where a position of special assistant to the dean of the faculty was created to oversee gender equity issues (Wilson, 2003).

A significant indicator that an administration is committed to advancing women is the appointment of staff to an initiative, rather than the appointment of an ad hoc committee, or the request that a faculty member lead the initiative as part of his or her service duties to the institution. For example, when the president of one university decided that gender and racial inclusiveness would be one of the university's highest priorities, he created a diversity advisory council, which he chaired. The council studied the situation and issued a statement acknowledging that the university was not doing well in this area. Each of five working groups made recommendations, which the council then began to implement. They collected best practices, so that colleagues would know what practices worked in one department or college. The president hoped that the success of women undergraduates would be noted and given high priority by other departments. The council also discussed making diversity a component of the performance evaluation of deans.

Finally, signaling can take the form of offering special incentives or resources for hiring female faculty. Institutions have also established targeted hiring initiatives or faculty recruiting programs and incentives to support them.[1] For example, one university adopted a hiring initiative to respond to strategic opportunities for increasing hires of women and targeted minorities. The program also included spousal hiring. Each school or college developed an internal process for implementing the program. Over a four-year time period, about 27 percent of faculty hired in the biological and physical sciences were women.

---

[1]In at least one case, the institution (University of Nebraska) was directed by the state to increase the percentage of women and minority faculty members (Anonymous, 2003).

Modifying or Expanding Faculty Recruitment Programs

Some institutions have chosen to tackle the problem of how to hire more female faculty by modifying or expanding their faculty recruitment programs.[2] Universities have taken such steps as

- *Engaging in focused faculty recruiting.* Institutions made recruiting for women and minorities a priority for some positions in addition to the normal availability of faculty positions.
- *Providing incentive grants.* One institution visited provided funds targeted for new women faculty hires. This institution found, however, that because no departmental investment was built into these grants, the impact of this initiative was not lasting. The institution required the department to provide some matching funds, ensuring departmental investment in ensuring the success of the faculty member. Similar steps were taken at Duke University, whose president recently announced that the university would "spend $1 million per year, indefinitely, to 'enhance the strategic hiring of women and minorities'" (Wilson, 2003).
- *Taking steps to diversify search committees.* It may be helpful if a search committee presents a more diverse face to the candidates and it strengthens a university's claim for striving for diversity. Such a strategy also broadens the network to scout potential candidates.
- *Casting a broader net to identify candidates.* Some institutions required search committees to delve more deeply into the pool of candidates before going forward with invitations for job talks. At one of the private universities, no search was permitted to go forward unless a qualified, credible female or minority candidate was included in the short list and invited to give a job talk. According to the members of this institution, this policy had positive effects. One was that the search committee conducted a much more thorough search than it might have otherwise. Usually, in addition to considering the applicants for an announced position, search committees relied on personal networks with colleagues at other institutions. To find additional candidates, search committee members asked whether colleagues making recommendations could also suggest women or minority candidates. This request usually resulted in the emergence of several qualified candidates. However, it was noted that these names came forth only when search members specifically requested such candidates.
- Valian (2004:217) offers several strategies for broadening the net. First, even though top-tier institutions "do not want to hire people from lower-tier institutions," more women are located in lower-tier institu-

---

[2]See, for example, the practical steps suggested by the University of Wisconsin ADVANCE Program (2005).

tions, and because productivity and location may be related, candidates from low-tier institutions may be even better than they look, especially if they are outperforming typical productivity for their location. Second, institutions should go out of their way to attract underrepresented faculty, which may be as simple as faculty at the hiring institution personally contacting peers at institutions. Third, universities can write job descriptions in a way that encourages women, among others, to apply.

• *Having institutional executives intervene.* If the current approach to hiring faculty is not producing increases in diversity, then that approach could be modified by, perhaps, calling for greater oversight by deans.

• *Collecting statistics on hiring processes and outcomes to aid in assessments.* Departments could collect data on each search by gender. Such data could include the number of candidates, number of candidates interviewed, number of offers, and number of hires. In addition, departments could collect data on the composition of their search committees, which could then be aggregated to the level of the school. The University of Pennsylvania's 2003 report, "Gender Equity: Penn's Second Annual Report," is an example of such data (University of Pennsylvania, 2003).[3]

Improving Institutional Policies and Practices

Institutions could adopt various policies and practices that would make them more attractive to prospective candidates of either gender (Sullivan et al., 2004).[4] These policies and practices include the following:

• *Extending the tenure clock.* One associate dean noted that childbirth used to be a "big impediment" in the careers of women, who were discouraged from taking time off. Now, however, faculty policies specify that any faculty member who wants an extension of the tenure clock to allow time off after childbirth may request it directly from the provost, and approval is expected. Extensions are not limited by the number of children or the gender of the parent. Obtaining a tenure clock extension for any other reason is said to be very difficult. Extension of the tenure clock is discussed more fully in Chapter 5.

• *Establishing parental leave policies and child care.* The dean at one university established a parental leave rule that allows either parent to take paid leave for one quarter. Another university examined the status of

---

[3]For links to this report and other research university gender equity reports, see http://www7.nationalacademies.org/cwse/gender_faculty_links.html. Accessed April 28, 2005.

[4]See Ward and Wolf-Wendel (2004) for a discussion of some reasons why it is difficult to establish or use such policies. See Quinn et al. (2004) for a list of recommendations of how to overcome the problems that often result from family-friendly policies.

child care through the joint efforts of a university committee and an office on child care.

> I'm proud to say we have transformed the two-body problem into a two-body opportunity. You find out that smart professional people marry smart professional people.
>
> —*Provost, during site visit*

• *Creating spousal hiring programs.* A large number of faculty members are married to other professionals, many of whom are also academics. Wolf-Wendel et al. (2003:163) suggest six broad approaches to helping the spouses and partners of faculty members find suitable jobs: offering relocation assistance, hiring a spouse or partner into an administrative position, hiring a spouse or partner into a non-tenure-track position, creating a shared position, creating a joint position with a nearby institution, or creating a tenure-track position for the spouse or partner.[5] This kind of program was being used by the university not located in a large metropolitan area because the lower percentage of potential employers reduced employment prospects for the spouse or partner. Of course, efforts to hire both spouses or partners depend to some extent on what each one does professionally. It is possible to offer a shared position to two physicists. Hiring two faculty in two different departments requires coordinating the efforts of those departments or of two different institutions.

• *Instituting sexual harassment sensitivity programs.* During the site visits, many people pointed out that within each discipline certain academic departments have reputations for being receptive or not receptive to women. To improve the climate of a department for current faculty and to aid in recruiting women faculty, some institutions have taken steps to combat sexual harassment. At each institution the committee raised the issue of sexual harassment. Most institutions responded that they have in place policies against sexual harassment and programs designed to educate employees. At some institutions the policies were buttressed by personal meetings with a dean or other member of the administration. Some institutions also have implemented pay equity reviews and conducted periodic salary equity studies to determine the comparability of compensation among faculty.

Improving the Positions of Candidates

Doctorate-producing institutions must assume some of the burden for enhancing the recruitment of female faculty. They need to do the best

---

[5]For a discussion of the problem and possible solutions, also see McNeil and Sher (1999).

job they can to outfit their graduates as candidates with high-quality credentials and recommendations. Actions that doctorate-granting institutions have taken to improve their own graduates include

- improving doctoral/postdoctoral training, including on conducting individual research and grant writing;
- ensuring that doctorates and postdoctorates are included in published research endeavors;
- directing women toward career resources provided by the institution, professional associations, and other entities;
- offering career advising and mentoring; and
- encouraging networking, because during a hiring season access to informal knowledge is often as important as finding job announcements.[6]

CONCLUSION

Many women have the prerequisites to be successful faculty. Of those who seek employment in academia, as opposed to employment in industry or the government, many have ambitions to be at the top institutions. One problem facing such women is that some of the challenges of achieving academic employment hit the average female doctorate and potential job candidate harder than the average male doctorate.

The challenges include negative reinforcement during graduate school, negative perceptions about the quality and likelihood of successful academic employment, and a tougher time in the hiring process. Those challenges, combined with the many more male applicants for positions, have resulted in fewer women in top academic institutions, despite the fact that so many women have the necessary credentials.

---

[6]One starting point is NETWORKING—*Why You Need to Know People Who Know People* by Patricia Rankin and Joyce Nielsen (2004).

BOX 4-3
Summary of Strategies for Recruiting Women Faculty

What faculty can do:

- Offer career advice and mentoring to doctoral and postdoctoral students.
- Assist doctoral and postdoctoral students in compiling a strong application package.

What department chairs can do:

- Create an image of the department as female friendly.
- Communicate with faculty about the importance of diversity in recruiting.
- Make departmental policies and practices transparent.
- Encourage faculty to work with doctoral and postdoctoral students for career placement and support their efforts.
- Diversify search committees.
- Evaluate and broaden efforts to publicize position openings.
- Identify ways to limit service requirements for junior faculty.

What deans and provosts can do:

- Communicate with department chairs about the importance of diversity in recruiting.
- Review policies on tenure clock, child care, leave, and spousal hiring. Policies could be made transparent.
- Conduct an assessment of recent hiring efforts and outcomes.
- Get involved in departmental searches.
- Institute human resources programs on sexual and racial discrimination.
- Evaluate recent departmental job offers for fairness in allocation of resources and salary.
- Consider the feasibility of special hiring slots for female faculty.
- Offer incentives to departments that are more inclusive.

What presidents can do:

- Publicly state the institution's commitment to diversity and inclusiveness whenever possible.
- Create an institutional structure, such as a standing committee, to address diversity issues within the faculty. Charge that committee with monitoring diversity across the institution and with making recommendations to increase diversity.
- Demonstrate the institution's commitment by meeting with faculty, encouraging the use of resources to enhance hiring strategies, and examining the institution's policies and practices on faculty issues.

5

Advancing Women Faculty

This chapter explores the challenges confronting female faculty who have successfully been hired into tenure-track positions and strategies for dealing with these challenges. Academics appointed to tenure-track positions have three major changes in status: (1) moving from tenure track to tenure; (2) moving from assistant professor to associate professor (sometimes these first two changes occur at the same time); and (3) moving from associate professor to full professor. Traditionally, those on the tenure track who expect to be or are denied tenure often leave their universities for positions elsewhere. Moving from associate professor to full professor is not always a requirement of tenure. Some faculty remain associate professors. The next step is to make sure these faculty advance, receive tenure, and ultimately receive a promotion to full professor. There are fewer women in senior faculty ranks across all disciplines (NRC, 2001).

CHALLENGES

Four challenges confront female faculty: (1) lower tenure and promotion rates, (2) longer time to promotion, (3) lower retention rates, and (4) lower job satisfaction. Taken together, these challenges diminish the probability that female faculty will remain at a university, lower the efficiency and productivity of faculty, and make an academic career less satisfying.

Lower Tenure and Promotion Rates

Studies have suggested that women are less likely than men to receive tenure or a promotion. Nationally, for science and engineering (S&E) doctorates working in academia, the likelihood of tenure was lower for women (NRC, 2001). In a more recent analysis of national data collected by the National Science Foundation (NSF), women were several percentage points less likely than men to be tenured and less likely to be promoted to senior ranks (NSF, 2004a). Other studies, focusing on specific fields, found that female academic biochemists were less likely to be promoted than male ones (Long et al., 1993), and women faculty in medicine were less likely than male faculty to attain the rank of full professor (Ash et al., 2004).[1]

Longer Time to Promotion

According to one study, across all fields (S&E and non-S&E) except for engineering and mathematics/statistics, women must wait longer to attain tenure. Significant differences in which men were favored were found in the biological sciences and psychology and the social sciences. Interestingly, in engineering women were significantly more likely to receive tenure first (Astin and Cress, 2003). Elsewhere, a study of physician faculty of U.S. medical schools found that women were "much less likely than men to have been promoted to associate professor or full professor rank after a median of 11 years of faculty service" (Tesch et al., 1995).

Interviewees at the sites visited echoed these broader trends. A college of engineering report at one university noted that women either left or were promoted at a slower rate than men. According to a dean of engineering at another school, women faculty are slower to be promoted than men, and retention is not as good. "They have yet to tenure a woman, and I'm getting ready to leave," said a chemist with good grants and teaching awards. A physicist observed that she was "the only tenured professor in the hard sciences." Another aspect of the situation was perhaps best summed up by a dean of the college of sciences who said that, despite changes, the academic community still has a traditional bias against young women who interrupt their careers to start a family.

---

[1]A new study of academics using the Survey of Doctoral Recipients from 1973-2001, suggests that there is no gender difference in the promotion to tenure or full professor in the sciences overall (Ginther and Kahn, 2006). This study differs from earlier studies in that it excludes the social sciences.

Lower Retention Rates

Data on female faculty retention rates are mixed. One study found that female faculty have higher attrition rates than male faculty both before and after tenure (August and Waltman, 2004). On the other hand, "statements by college and university presidents, deans, and department heads that it is impossible to retain highly qualified female science and engineering faculty members in their institutions led to a study conducted at The Henry Luce Foundation. The unpublished data submitted by more than 180 colleges and universities reveal that the retention rates of faculty members hired into tenure-track positions in the physical sciences, mathematics, and computer science over the past 15 years, are virtually identical for women and men (73%)" (Rosser and Daniels, 2004:133).

Lower Job Satisfaction

There is some evidence that, in general, women are less satisfied in the academic workplace than men and are more likely to leave academia during the first seven years (Trower and Chait, 2002). A consequence of lower satisfaction may be unhappiness in the profession, which in turn may lead to lower productivity, lower retention rates, and a reduced pool of future academics. Indeed, one concern is that "unhappiness gets transmitted to younger women starting out and may help scare a new generation away from academia" (Lawler, 1999).

An important point is that women are more likely to perceive career impediments that have a gender component. In fact, one study based on a 1990 survey of selected full-time faculty at the School of Medicine at Johns Hopkins University (Fried et al., 1996) recorded a variety of negative perceptions for women. For example, 52 percent of women and 18 percent of men surveyed, agreed with the statement: "There are gender-based obstacles in my division to career success and satisfaction of women." Seventy five percent of women and 32 percent of men agreed with the following statement: "Men have difficulty taking careers of women faculty seriously and accepting women as colleagues." Finally, 10 percent of women and 2 percent of men agreed with the statement: "I have been harassed sexually on the job." A larger study of faculty in academic medicine by Carr et al. (2000) reached similar conclusions (Table 5-1). These two studies suggest that female faculty are conscious of gender-based obstacles—to whatever extent they exist.

UNDERLYING CAUSES OF CHALLENGES

Several causes may underlie these four challenges: inadequate protection of research time; fewer institutional resources devoted to women

TABLE 5-1 Perception and Experience of Discrimination and Harassment by Gender

Problem[a]	Adjusted Mean Value[b] (Percent)		Adjusted Means (95% CD)[c]	
	Women (n=953)	Men (n=1010)	Percentage Points	p value
Respondents who perceived gender-specific bias in the academic environment[d]	11	90	47 (43-52)	<0.001
Respondents who personally experienced gender bias in professional advancement[e]	60	9	51 (48-55)	<0.001
Respondents who personally experienced gender advantage in professional advancement	31	11	20 (16-23)	<0.001
Respondents who personally experienced harassment[f]	52	5	47 (44-50)	<0.001

[a]Each question was scored on a scale of 1 to 5. Responses of 3, 4, or 5 were counted as positive.
[b]Adjusted for medical school, specialty, ethnicity/race or minority, and years since first faculty appointment.
[c]Value for women minus the value for men.
[d]1 = no, never, 5 = yes, frequently
[e]1 = no, 2 = not to my knowledge, 3 = possibly, 4 = probably, 5 = yes
[f]1 = number 2 = yes.
SOURCES: Carr et. al (2000).

than to men; work-family conflicts; and an alienating departmental culture.

Inadequate Protection of Research Time

All faculty must balance among three principal professional activities: research, teaching, and service.[2] Together, these activities form the experience on which faculty are judged in tenure and promotion deci-

---

[2]More precisely, in its National Survey of Postsecondary Faculty (NSOPF), the Department of Education asks respondents to break down their work time by estimating the percentage of time spent on (and, separately, the percentage of time the respondent would prefer to spend on) teaching undergraduate students, teaching graduate students, research/scholarship, professional growth, administration, service, and other work, including consulting, freelance work, and other non-teaching professional activities.

> In the sciences, women have a more challenging set of expectations, especially faculty early in their career. Certain milestones need to be passed as a function of time—number of publications and so on. And if a person misses one, it's not positive. These are rules made by the boys. It's a challenge for women because of family responsibilities they may have.
>
> —*Dean, during site visit*

sions. At major research universities, research is often given more weight than the other two categories. Protecting research time, in an inverse relationship with rank, is critical for faculty: the more junior faculty need the most research time.

It is asserted in the literature that women face more alternative commitments for their time than men. These commitments—from both inside and outside the university setting—reduce the amount of time women can spend on research, and thus lower their probability of advancing through the ranks of academia. Within the university setting, women accept or are assigned more service tasks or more demanding teaching duties. Women may be more likely to end up as mentors and advisers; they may be asked to serve on many committees to make the committees more diverse; and they may be less likely to say no (Fogg, 2003a). Outside the university, women have more parental duties that can cut into research time.

Interviewees at one university noted that there was too much advising and committee work, which take away time for research. The chair of an engineering department pointed out the fortitude of women needs to be higher than that of men, because the pressures are greater on women to serve on many committees and serve as mentors. Overall, interviewees suggested that the differential tendency for women faculty members to mentor, volunteer, and otherwise be a "good citizen" may hold women back academically.

Fewer Institutional Resources

A second cause of the challenges facing women is that female faculty may receive less institutional support and resources than male faculty. A 1999 Massachusetts Institute of Technology (MIT) study found that "in some departments, men and women faculty appeared to share equally in material resources and rewards, in others they did not. Inequitable distributions were found involving space, amount of nine-month salary paid from individual research grants, teaching assignments, awards and distinctions, inclusion on important committees and assignments within the department." Although it is difficult to measure gender disparities in institutional resource allocation, one exception is salaries, because of the many studies conducted comparing women's salaries to men's. In academia, women at comparable levels tend to receive lower salaries than men (Ginther, 2001, 2004; NRC, 2001). The salary gap has, however, diminished over time, and academic salaries are affected by many factors, including demographic and employer characteristics and the academic activities of faculty. Again, these national trends were reflected in the experiences recounted by the interviewees.

Work-Family Conflicts

The conflict between managing family and work is often called the greatest problem facing female faculty. Women, who are frequently mothers and primary caregivers, face more pressures to balance professional activities and home life demands. An MIT study (1999) found that work and family pressures could be difficult to manage, particularly for the junior faculty: "Junior women faculty felt included and supported in their departments. Their most common concern was the extraordinary difficulty of combining family and work."

Having children can place enormous pressures on female faculty. The evidence suggests that families tend to affect women negatively but men positively, as suggested by the results of one study by Mason and Goulden (2002): "In the sciences and engineering, among those working in academia, men who have early babies are strikingly more successful in earning tenure than women who have early babies." Similar findings appear in other research (NRC, 2001; NSF, 2004a).

Evidence collected during the site visits supported these concerns. For example, at one university a female department chair said, "The single biggest obstacle against progressing in academia is simple, overwork." She also pointed out that some women, especially those who want children, leave "because it's simply not possible to have two full-time careers and kids."

At another university one female faculty member reported a lack of sympathy for her child-care needs; meetings are often scheduled at times that either she or her husband has to take care of their child, and the expectation is that she will be the one to do that. Other faculty also reported child-care problems, such as being unable to attend meetings at times when child care is not available. Another described a general lack of consideration for parents, which he described as a problem nation-wide.

An Alienating Departmental Culture

A final cause of the challenges facing female faculty derives from historically male-oriented departmental and institutional norms and structures. A female-unfriendly work environment can produce female isolation or marginalization, which undermines the efforts of female faculty to obtain tenure or a promotion, and the possibility that different criteria are used to judge male and female faculty in tenure and promotion cases.

An extreme product of this culture can be harassment of female faculty. Harassment, including sexual harassment, occurs on university campuses to students, faculty, and staff. It is more likely to be directed at women. In a 1990 faculty survey conducted at the School of Medicine at Johns Hopkins University, 10 percent of the women surveyed indicated they had been sexually harassed on the job (Fried et al., 1996). Indeed, each year is likely to bring new media reports of harassment lawsuits involving universities and university personnel (Fogg, 2004; Wilson, 2004a). Yet some harassment may go unreported. Regardless of whether harassment is occurring on a campus, if several students or faculty members perceive it to be happening, then it is a challenge to women's retention and advancement.

Perhaps less obvious than harassment but no less important is the marginalization of women faculty on campuses. Not only should universities have sufficient percentages of women faculty, but they also should participate in the life of their field and in the university. The themes of marginalization (being excluded from positions or organizations of power) and isolation (being excluded from the scientific community) were raised in the context of the MIT report (1999), where "a common finding for most senior women faculty was that the women were 'invisible,' excluded from a voice in their departments and from positions of any real power. This 'marginalization' had occurred as the women progressed through their careers at MIT, making their jobs increasingly difficult and less satisfying."

Once the issue of isolation is raised, many women at higher education institutions acknowledge that it is a problem:

> Isolation is widely recognized as a problem for women in academic science, carrying with it a variety of negative consequences including stigma, depletion of self-confidence, and exclusion from access to informal sources of professional information. Informal networks are indispensable to professional development, career advancement, and the scientific process. Contiguity of helpful colleagues improves the conditions for scientific achievement; lack of sympathetic interaction lowers it. Isolated individuals not only lack social psychological support, but also the social capital, which underlies success. (Etzkowitz et al., 1994:52)

Interviewees at three of the four institutions visited felt that women were isolated at those institutions. One female professor said that her department tended to "hire really good women because they are really good women—but they have no connection with the rest of the department." The women were successful, but had no natural collaborators. Some male students at another institution visited did not want the reputation of including women in their study groups. At a third university one faculty member said she had no female peers to talk to, because the two other female colleagues were senior to her.[3]

Yet another problem is different kinds of evaluations being applied to female and male faculty. This problem could manifest itself in two ways. First, if female faculty face harder criteria from external reviewers for publications or grants, then their productivity might be lower, which would in turn translate into a more difficult tenure or promotion review. Second, if internal reviewers such as tenure and promotion committees review women using criteria different from those used for men, women may find it more difficult than men to advance in their careers. Persell (1983) found evidence that the quality of work had different effects on the careers of men than those of women. Quantity of work also had different effects: quantity counted less for men, who produced more publications, than for women, who produced fewer publications. However, Steinpreis et al. (1999) found that both men and women evaluated the curriculum vitae of tenure candidates equally—that is, they were equally likely to award tenure to male and female candidates, whom they rated similarly for teaching, research, and service.

BOX 5-1
Summary of Challenges

✓ Women faculty have lower rates of tenure and promotion.
✓ Women faculty must wait longer to receive a promotion.
✓ Women faculty have lower rates of retention.
✓ Women faculty have lower job satisfaction.

---

[3]The danger for a department with few women is that if women faculty prefer a department with more women, they may leave for such departments. The department of chemistry at Rutgers University has admitted encouraging women to come to Rutgers for this reason (McGinn, 2005).

STRATEGIES

As noted earlier, at the universities visited the percentage of women faculty recruited has increased, indicating the success of the programs and changes that these institutions have put into place. Most of the programs involved efforts to increase the percentage of women in applicant pools or to improve the climate for women faculty on campus. Many of these programs, such as child care, potentially benefit all faculty.

BOX 5-2
Strategies for Advancing Women Faculty

✓ Have the institution and departments signal the importance of women.
✓ Create and reinforce female-friendly policies.
✓ Strengthen mentoring.
✓ Engage women faculty more fully in the institution.

Signaling the Importance of Women

At the institutions visited, top administrators very publicly supported the goal of advancing women and acted on their statements. Interviewees at one university felt that the dean and provost were critical to increasing women faculty participation at the top, because they can influence new hiring and provide funding. General approaches are implemented by an institution, but often the impetus for the change originated with an individual, usually one with the power at the institution to lead, set, and enforce policy.

As noted earlier, interviewees attributed recent progress at one university to many different forces and individuals over the past two decades, but also to the fact that the current provost was determined to hire more women. It was the provost who oversaw the first gender equity pay exercise in the early 1990s and a follow-up study toward the end of the 1990s.

Department chairs play a critical role in a faculty member's career. For women faculty, especially when a woman is the first woman in that department or school, the demand for committee service can be very high, especially at those institutions seeking to increase women faculty. In such situations the chair can play an important role in shielding junior faculty from excessive requests. Because the chair also determines teaching assignments, he or she can work to ensure that no one faculty member has to shoulder an undue burden in both teaching load and rotation.

Teaching load encompasses the number of courses taught, the number of course preparations (i.e., the number of different courses taught), and course level (e.g., undergraduate versus graduate). For example, a young faculty member who is asked to teach substantively different courses every year will likely

> It's the chairs and the deans who set the climate.
>
> —*Faculty member, during site visit*

spend more time on course development than faculty members given the same or similar courses to teach regularly.

Creating and Reinforcing Policies and Practices

Institutions can adopt various policies and practices to enhance or ease the advancement of female faculty. Extending the tenure clock, a popular policy described in detail in Chapter 5, is only one part of the solution, however. Recent studies have found that female faculty are hesitant to make use of such a policy, because many women fear that taking an extension will hurt their career—an effect not conclusively documented (Bhattacharjee, 2004). Universities must therefore identify ways to both encourage this practice when appropriate and take steps to ensure that faculty are not punished for taking advantage of the policy. An initial step is to make tenure policies more transparent to all faculty.

Other policies and practices that help to retain and advance women faculty are the following:

• *Reinforcing parental leave policies and child care.* One institution formed a task force on child care. Some of the initiatives were (1) continuing exploration of the relationship between employment conditions for child-care workers, university or union-based support for campus child care, and parent tuition payments; (2) expanding care for low-income parents; and (3) expanding infant, sick child, and extended hours care. At the time the university had seven child-care centers on campus.

• *Reinforcing sexual harassment sensitivity programs.* Support of sexual harassment policies should be reinforced regularly and widely publicized. Some institutions provide an ombudsperson to channel cases of sexual harassment.

• *Limiting service among junior faculty.* The school of engineering at one university attempted to improve retention by changing the notion that all assistant professors are alike and follow the same track. "We need personalization," said an associate dean. "People find their success on a personal, individual track." One department made a conscious effort to shield junior faculty from administrative duties during their early years to help avoid burnout. The president of another university announced that one woman was granted tenure primarily because of her role as a mentor and teacher. This represents an alternative approach: if time for research cannot be increased, the weight of teaching and service can be increased instead.

• *Undertaking periodic reviews and adjustments of salaries.* One university undertook a gender pay equity exercise a decade after its first. In all, over a third of those reviewed received a gender pay equity adjustment. Many other universities conduct salary equity reviews, using different models to determine whether male and female employees working in similar jobs are receiving similar pay. The strategy thus has two parts: conducting a self-assessment and, when inequity is revealed, raising salaries appropriately. The process should be repeated periodically.

• *Changing day-to-day policies.* Some policies involving day-to-day activities can be easily altered to make working conditions much better. One example is changing the time of standing meetings, so that faculty with family responsibilities (often women) are more easily able to participate (Fried et al., 1996).

• *Allowing modified duties.* Sullivan et al. (2004) notes that some universities have mechanisms to temporarily reduce a faculty member's duties—teaching, research, or service—without a reduction in pay. "Teaching demands often make it difficult for faculty to use traditional sick or disability leave; modified duties policies provide an alternative type of leave that allows them time to care for newborns, newly adopted or fostered children, or critically ill spouses, partners, or parents without completely removing themselves from the campus for an extended period. For women faculty members recovering from childbirth, a modified duties policy can be seen as equivalent to the six to eight weeks of paid full-time sick or disability leave for childbirth that most universities offer to women in staff positions."

Sullivan et al. (2004) conclude by noting that successful universities "(1) formalize their policies and make them entitlements; (2) continually educate faculty and administrators about the policies; (3) address issues that discourage faculty from using work-family benefits; (4) use data to promote programs that support balance between work and family; and (5) foster collaboration between champions of individual policies and relevant institutional committees."

Strengthening Mentoring

The institutions visited had the means in place to mentor young faculty through tenure. Some of these efforts were informal—a senior faculty member would provide advice and suggestions when asked by a junior faculty member. Other efforts were more formal—a guidance committee would track progress and support the junior faculty member through tenure. The committee approach, because it has been formalized, may provide more consistent guidance to all junior faculty, and it is beneficial to both the individual and the department.

> The key to success for women is in putting a lot of thought into the mentoring system.
>
> —*Faculty member, during site visit*

Mentoring should be provided by faculty other than those in oversight positions, such as department chairs, to avoid awkward mentoring relationships. The chairs of larger departments also simply do not have time to mentor all new or young faculty. Mentoring only a few faculty members could be perceived as favoritism, leading to conflict within the department. Other faculty, however, play enormously important roles as mentors and role models, and in setting the climate.

For many faculty, the department is the professional setting for an entire career, and colleagues are a critical component of that setting. Although fellow faculty can provide guidance and insight to successful tenure at that institution, many women faculty reported that being the only woman or one of few women in a department led to feelings of isolation. Related to that finding, one university's approach to mentoring began with a study commissioned by the chancellor in the 1980s that revealed that nontenured women faculty were voluntarily resigning from the university at a rate greater than that of their male counterparts. Many women cited feelings of isolation as a major reason for their departure. A program devoted to mentoring women faculty was adopted and expanded to include additional resources and services for tenured women. In the fall of each year, all newly hired and newly tenured women were invited to participate in the program. Each nontenured woman was matched with a tenured woman outside her own department but in her field. Faculty valued the ability to discuss difficult issues with someone who was not part of the same department. The program, which complemented the traditional departmental adviser function, offered an annual orientation meeting, advisory committees meetings, a reception for mentors and mentees, and a brown bag series featuring discussions on teaching, balancing personal and professional commitments, the spousal hire program, and many other topics.

Many departments and colleges have their own mentoring programs for women faculty. Recently, one of the engineering colleges visited conducted a small survey of assistant professors about the college's mentoring program. Interviewees indicated that they were generally satisfied, although they said the quality of the mentoring was highly variable. Some were extremely satisfied, finding a close collegial relationship, outstanding collaboration or involvement, and active assistance in areas such as obtaining research funding or good graduate students. At least two were dissatisfied with the mentoring, citing mainly the poor advice they had received. Based on that survey, a college of engineering committee recommended a significant change: separation of the mentoring and evaluation/oversight functions. It also recommended that junior faculty members be allowed to choose their mentor or mentoring committee.

Engaging Female Faculty More Fully in the Institution

Institutions should take steps to ensure that female faculty feel as though they belong and are contributing to the institution. Some chairs might respond by simply putting female faculty on every committee possible. Serving on some committees, especially those that have some power over policy making is helpful, but membership in too many committees overemphasizes service at the expense of research and teaching. Yet female faculty should be included in (or asked to lead) all the more informal activities in the department, such as brown bag lectures and colloquia. Faculty achievements should be rewarded with equal levels of recognition.

CONCLUSION

By most accounts, female faculty appear to advance along the academic career pathway more slowly than males. Most studies suggest that women are less likely to receive tenure or a promotion and tend to spend more time in lower ranks. Partly as a result, female faculty are less satisfied and more likely than their male counterparts to change jobs or move out of academia. The underlying causes behind these outcomes include working conditions that have more negative effects on women than on men and evaluations that appear, unintentionally or otherwise, to undervalue women's efforts and accomplishments compared with male faculty.

Admittedly, it is easier to change institutional policies and practices than it is to change the direction of decision making. However, many steps can be taken to ensure that working conditions affect the different kinds of faculty similarly. Indeed, additional oversight may guarantee that tenure and promotion committees treat all faculty fairly. Ultimately, however, each person participating in these processes must commit himself or herself to administering equitable treatment.

BOX 5-3
Summary of Strategies for Advancing Women Faculty

What faculty can do:

- Treat women faculty respectfully as equal colleagues.
- Be wary of unintentional thinking based on gender schemas.

What department chairs can do:

- Create an image of the department as female-friendly.
- Where possible, modify existing departmental policies and practices—for example, selecting times for standing meetings—so that no type of faculty member is disproportionately affected.
- Make departmental policies and practices transparent.
- Assess the distribution of institutional resources such as lab space and research assistants for fairness.
- Put women on important departmental committees and recommend female faculty for important school-wide or university-wide committees.
- Develop mentoring programs for all faculty.
- Identify ways to limit service requirements for junior faculty.

What deans and provosts can do:

- Communicate with department chairs about the importance of diversity.
- Review policies on tenure clock, child care, leave, and spousal hiring. Policies could be made transparent.
- Conduct an assessment of diversity within departments.
- Reinforce human resources programs on sexual and racial discrimination.
- Evaluate recent departmental offers for fairness in allocation of resources and salary.
- Offer incentives to departments that are more inclusive.

What presidents can do:

- Publicly state the institution's commitment to diversity and inclusiveness whenever possible.
- Create an institutional structure, such as a standing committee, to address diversity issues within the faculty. Charge that committee with monitoring diversity across the institution and with making recommendations to increase diversity.
- Demonstrate the institution's commitment by meeting with faculty and devoting resources to programs that assist female students and faculty.

6

Advancing Women to Executive Positions

When the Committee on Women in Science and Engineering first examined the issue of women in top administrative positions—presidents, chancellors, provosts, and deans—women were scarcely to be found. That situation has improved remarkably today. As one report put it, women presidents are no longer an anomaly and are now merely a minority (Brown et al., 2001b). Currently, women are presidents, provosts, and deans across a range of universities and colleges, including community colleges, liberal arts colleges, the Ivy League, and other research universities. However, the challenge of moving more women into these positions still remains.

The relatively few women who do make it into administration also serve as important role models. Judy Hample, chancellor of the Pennsylvania State System, has pointed out that the presence of a female or a nonwhite in the president's office "sends a signal [to prospective students] that the campus environment is friendly to women and minorities in a way that brochures and everything else could not send" (quoted in Schackner, 2005). Indeed, when women hold some of the top jobs at a university, they inspire women at all levels of the university, including faculty and students, by demonstrating that women can do as good a job as men. It may also be the case that women bring unique qualities to the job. Thus as traditional outsiders, women executives may be better able to champion inclusiveness policies and practices.

CHALLENGES

Much like the decisions to attend college, major in science or engineering (S&E), and apply for an academic position, pursuing a high-ranking administrator position at a university is a choice. Prospective candidates are already employed: candidates for presidential positions may be provosts; candidates for dean positions may be departmental chairs or faculty (Lively, 2000b.) Moreover, the decision by a university board of trustees to offer a candidate a position is also a choice. The interaction of these two decisions determines the number of men and women in top executive positions at universities. If women are less interested in applying for such positions, or if university decision makers are less interested in choosing a female candidate, then the number of women top administrators will be low.

"Improving but low" is a phrase that best characterizes the current situation. There seems to be many more qualified female candidates than the number of women in administrative positions (Lively, 2000a, b; Rivard, 2003). Lively (2000b:34) notes

> Many elite universities, particularly private ones, didn't even accept female students or begin hiring female professors in significant numbers until the late 1960's.

> Those were the years when most of the current female provosts earned their Ph.D.'s and found jobs as assistant professors. During the late 70's, the 80's, and the early 90's, they earned tenure, became full professors, and went on to serve as department chairwomen, deans, and in other posts that allowed them to demonstrate their administrative talents. By the mid to late 1990's, there were enough well-credentialed women in the right kinds of jobs to provide search committees with the pools necessary to name some as provosts.

"Today, only one in five college presidents is a woman, despite the fact that 40 percent of faculty and administrators are women. Clearly, the pipeline is primed" (Van Ummersen, 2001). As noted in Chapter 4 on faculty recruitment, the issue of recruiting more women faculty has moved beyond the "pipeline" metaphor, and now focuses on whether prospective women faculty might face other obstacles. This finding should serve as a useful reminder to recruiters to consider whether the only obstacle to a greater presence of women among top university leadership is simply the lack of enough qualified women. Moreover, the major research universities have lower percentages of women in top jobs than other types of higher education institutions. The American Council on Education (ACE) conducts the American College President Study. In 2001 it found that, overall, 21 percent of college and university presidents were female. Twenty-seven percent of presidents at two-year colleges were female, but only 12 percent of presidents at doctorate-granting institutions were female.

These statistics were borne out to the committee during its site visits. Even in noteworthy institutions, women were largely absent from positions such as dean or department chair. At one university visited, at the highest levels—deans, provost, and chancellor—most administrators were male. The provost admitted that he did not "feel too good about it." He said that two recent senior administration searches had come down to several female and male candidates and that the male was chosen in both searches. By placing women in top administrative positions, universities may be able to inspire women students and faculty and therefore increase the chances that women faculty are recruited and advanced.

The fact that there are growing numbers of women qualified to hold administrative positions, but relatively few do so— particularly in major research universities, may be explained by one of two possibilities. One possibility is that various types of higher education institutions have to be treated differently because they have different applicant pools, and women are less likely to be found in the pools for major research universities. The other possibility is that there is one large applicant pool and that some other factor is tending to hinder women's advancement in the major research universities.

A number of researchers have offered suggestions about what that other factor might be. One issue that complicates the answer is that at times the same candidate takes a top administrative job at different schools at different times. As a result, the number of women in such positions appears larger because a few women are rotating through jobs at different institutions. (However, the number of institutions that have had female top administrators would then rise.)

The pipeline issue aside, what other factors may explain the current dearth of women leaders? One factor is that institutions have broadened the search for top administrators in ways that unintentionally reduce the odds that a woman will succeed. Increasingly universities are turning to candidates outside of higher education—that is, prospective leaders whose immediate prior position was not in academia. In 2001, 15 percent of presidents fell into this category. The concern is that a broader applicant pool that includes individuals from outside of academia might contain a lot more male candidates.

A second factor is that women are less interested in such positions than in others because the benefits are lower for women, and the costs, such as the workload, are higher. Indeed, women presidents are distinguished by more than their gender. According to the *Chronicle of Higher Education*, in 2001 only four women were among the top 50 presidents with the largest compensation packages (Nicklin, 2001).

A third factor is discrimination. Search committees may be less in-clined to hire a woman for president because of "concerns about her abilities to work closely with a predominantly male faculty and senior management team; 'style' issues that are less demonstrable than experi-ence and ability; and, in the case of minority women, hidden reservations toward females and people of color" (Haro, 1991). One report suggested that boards prefer to hire married candidates—and as noted above, more male candidates than women candidates, in percentage terms, are likely to be married (Brown et al., 2001b).

BOX 6-1
Summary of Challenges

There are fewer women top administrators than might be expected by simply viewing the proportion of senior women.

✓ The pipeline may still be small.
✓ Universities are increasingly searching in areas dominated by male candi-dates.
✓ Women may show less interest in top administration positions, because they perceive the job to be less satisfying or to offer fewer rewards.
✓ Discrimination may hinder the advancement of women.

STRATEGIES

President Shirley Tilghman of Princeton University has asked, "When will people stop making note of the fact that the newly appointed presi-dent of university X is a woman? When will we feel as though we have hit a critical mass so that this is just not noticeable anymore?"(quoted in Zernike, 2001). This section describes the strategies that may be effective in advancing women to executive positions.

BOX 6-2
Strategies for Recruiting and Advancing
Women to Executive Positions

✓ Conduct an institutional audit.
✓ Mentor "presidents-in-training."
✓ Develop executive leadership training.
✓ Engage in networking activities.
✓ Change the search process.

Conducting an Institutional Audit

Brown et al. (2002) suggest a useful early step for education institutions wishing to recruit women for top administrative positions: conduct a leadership development audit of the institution. Such an audit is designed to answer the following questions:

- What leadership positions do women currently hold in the faculty administration and board?
- What proportion of the institution's leaders are women?
- What role do women leaders play in formal and informal decision-making processes?
- Are the women leaders viewed as leaders of men and women, or only as leaders of women? How can women leaders be supported to lead diverse constituencies?
- Are leadership and development opportunities available for everyone at all levels of the institution?
- Does faculty development include development of leadership skills, not just skills related to a discipline? (Brown et al., 2002:15)[1]

These kinds of questions could also be asked in a comparative way, across similar higher education institutions. These questions remind recruiters to focus on all the potential candidates for executive positions rather than the narrower set of individuals who have already succeeded in obtaining a leadership position.[2]

Mentoring "Presidents-in-Training"

According to Brown et al. (2001b:9), "most men and women college presidents agree that mentoring has played an important role in their careers." Female chairs, deans, and provosts need encouragement and advice, and they should actively seek it out. Likewise, female executives should consider mentoring women who could be presidential material. Basinger (2001) mentions that the Women Presidents Network of the American Association of State Colleges and Universities (AASCU) has joined forces with the National Council of Chief Academic Officers to

---

[1]Brown et al. (2002) describe some programs that support women in leadership positions.

[2]It might be interesting to conduct a study of candidates for top administrative jobs, comparing those who succeeded in landing such a position with those who did not (Santovec, 2004).

"begin linking female provosts interested in college presidencies with female presidents who will be mentors."

An example of a program that combines mentoring and leadership training is the ACE Fellows Program: "Selected men and women faculty and administrators aspiring to senior positions take a leave from their institutions (one year, one semester, or periodically) to intern with a president or vice president at another institution. Through observation and participation, Fellows learn about decision making; fostering relationships with state legislatures, business and industry, K-12, the broader community, and the governing board; relationships among administrative offices; and the nature of educational leadership, administrative organization, and change strategies" (Brown et al., 2001a:35).[3] Of course, not all administrators will go through such formal training programs. Many will gain experience through their other academic work experience. Thus, mentoring can happen formally or informally.

Developing Executive Leadership Training

The skill set needed to succeed as an executive within a higher education institution differs to some extent from the skill set needed to be a faculty member, or even a chair or dean. Potential candidates need expertise in areas such as administration, communication, conflict resolution, budget, legislation, and educational planning (Andruskiw and Howes, 1980). Executive leadership training can help women to gain that expertise. One type of training program invites women from many campuses to come together at one location. Another type of training program is run at one particular institution or institutional system for women within that area. One example of such a program is the AASCU's Millennium Leadership Initiative: "The Millennium Leadership Initiative (MLI) is a focused leadership development program designed to strengthen the preparation and eligibility of persons who are traditionally underrepresented in the roles of president or chancellor in our nation's colleges and universities."[4] Another example is the Summer Institute for Women in Higher Education Administration at Bryn Mawr College: "The Summer Institute offers women administrators and faculty intensive training in education administration. The curriculum prepares participants to work with issues currently facing higher education, with emphasis on the growing diver-

---

[3]Brown et al. (2001b) lists several examples of different programs that support women in leadership positions.

[4]For more on the Millennium Leadership Initiative, see http://www.aascu.org/mli/default.htm. Accessed March 29, 2005.

sity of the student body and the work force."[5] Training in negotiation is also helpful for female faculty and administrators, because there is some evidence that women are less assertive than men in negotiating.[6]

Such structured workshops and training are not the only approaches available to female faculty willing to move into administration; they can merely seek to talk to and observe the actions of administration leaders (Raines and Alberg, 2003). Other experiences could be gained through administrative internships or temporary administrative positions and serving on policy making or administrative committees.

Engaging in Networking

Female presidents may be more comfortable discussing issues with female peers: "In ways unlike those of male presidents before them, female presidents have sought one another out at national meetings of presidents say college leaders and education scholars. In recent years, some of them have formed more systematic strategies for staying in touch on a regular basis" (Basinger, 2001).

Examples of the networking efforts of women administrators include the Women Presidents Network of the AASCU (see Basinger, 2001) and the network of the American Council on Education, Office of Women in Higher Education, and its state affiliates:

> With a grant from the Carnegie Corporation in 1977, ACE's Office of Women in Higher Education (OWHE) started the ACE National Identification Program, which is now the ACE Network. Through the National Identification Program, OWHE aimed to address the needs of women and the issues relating to women's leadership in higher education. OWHE identified these needs and issues during its early years, through meetings with women faculty and administrators throughout the United States. . . . The ACE Network is a national system of networks within each state, Puerto Rico, and the District of Columbia. Each state network is led by a *state coordinator* who works with *institutional representatives* and at least one presidential sponsor to develop programs that identify, develop, advance, and support women in higher education careers within that state. In addition, members of the *Executive Board* of the ACE Network serve as advisers to OWHE, liaisons to the state networks, and mentors to state coordinators.[7]

---

[5]For more on the Summer Institute for Women in Higher Education Administration, see http://www.brynmawr.edu/summerinstitute/. Accessed March 29, 2005.

[6]See, for example, Babcock and Laschever (2003).

[7]Office of Women in Higher Education, The ACE Network, at http://www.acenet.edu/programs/owhe/network.cfm. Accessed March 29, 2005.

Changing the Search Process

The first step in changing the search process for women administrators is to appoint a diverse search committee: "The committee should reflect the diversity that the search claims to be seeking. If you want to attract a diverse candidate pool, it makes sense to start with a diverse committee. That will not guarantee a mixed slate of candidates, but it will increase the odds" (Dowdall, 2004). The second important step is to make sure that executive search firms, outside consultants, university trustees and boards, and the search committee all understand the importance of diversity. The third step is to attempt to cast a wider net. It is true that search committees are more likely to focus on men. Indeed, according to the assistant director of the Center for Policy Analysis at the American Council on Education, "Search committees at doctoral institutions are looking for folks with significant experience in leading complex institutions, and historically, that's been men and white men" (quoted in Basinger, 2002). However, there are many qualified female candidates for academic executive positions, and efforts to identify such candidates should be made from both the bottom-up and the top-down.

CONCLUSION

Women continue to achieve positions of leadership in the major research universities. Although their numbers remain lower than at other types of higher education institutions, the potential female pool for such positions is increasing. Women may face greater resistance either in being considered for leadership roles or in occupying those positions. Evaluators may be biased against women to varying degrees and for a variety of reasons, including the view that women lack the necessary skills. Universities and other organizations have taken steps to help remedy these problems.

BOX 6-3
**Summary of Strategies for Recruiting and Advancing Women
to Executive Positions**

What faculty can do:

- Aspire to leadership positions.
- Take advantage of opportunities, both on and off campus, to gain leadership experience.
- Network with other female faculty interested in leadership positions and with male and female academic officers.

What department chairs can do:

- Encourage female faculty to gain experience and skills in administration and to consider seeking administrative positions.
- Mentor female faculty on matters of administration.
- Create and use support networks (applicable to female department chairs).

What deans and provosts can do:

- Encourage female faculty to gain experience and skills in administration and to consider leadership positions.
- Conduct an institutional audit.
- Develop on-campus leadership programs for faculty.
- Mentor prospective academic officers.
- Create and use support networks (applicable to female deans and provosts).

What presidents can do:

- Publicly state the institution's commitment to diversity and inclusiveness whenever possible.
- Mentor prospective candidates for executive positions. Mentoring can be done at the same institution or across institutions.
- Conduct a self-assessment of the institution.
- Encourage prospective candidates to enroll in leadership training programs.
- Develop a leadership program on campus.
- Diversify search committees for departmental chair or dean positions.

7

Conclusion

During their site visits to the four universities, the committee found common themes and experiences across institutions, as well as approaches tailored to local situations. Both the public and private universities explored in this study shared an interest in fixing the pipeline that loses women as they move through the ranks of academia, in recruiting and retaining women, in expanding programs of interest for women in science and engineering (S&E), and in emphasizing data collection and research on gender equity issues.

Echoed throughout the visits was the view that, for most of the initiatives to succeed, the top members of an administration had to strongly and publicly support efforts to promote women in science and engineering. The institutions visited were widely publicizing their promotion of inclusiveness and support for women. For example, at one university a commitment to women's advancement was incorporated into the institution's strategic plan. The commitment to a diverse campus, both at the student and faculty level, was incorporated into the mission of the institutions. Indeed, all four universities seemed to be actively promoting an inclusive campus climate, and they had taken actions to support stated positions swiftly and publicized them. Even a simple change can be effective. One university found that moving the women in engineering program office next to that of the dean facilitated collaboration between office staffs and assured the program would not be lost among the myriad tasks facing the dean.

Another theme and an important component of the universities' policies—and in some ways a policy in itself—were the reports and studies undertaken by the universities to document and identify challenges and the effects of institutional policies. One university, for example, under-took two salary equity studies. With the assistance of federal grants, this university also established a center to gather data, monitor results, and disseminate information on the best practices for advancing women. Partly underlying the center's mission was the view that it was necessary and beneficial to the institution to attract more women and underrepre-sented minorities to careers in science, mathematics, and engineering.

Another university published an internal report on best practices for diversity. Some of the good practices identified were mentoring, a cen-tralized fund for minority recruiting, the inclusion of diversity in the strategic plans of departments, an incentive grants program for diversity efforts, and diversity advisory councils. "The report was well received," said a dean, "because it was not perceived as hammering people. It said we were doing well, what can we do better?"

A third university conducted a self-assessment within an individual school, which led to a study of its undergraduate students. In response to the study, the school made a series of changes, primarily in recruiting strategy, admissions criteria, and curriculum. Within four years the per-centage of women in the entering class had increased fivefold in that particular school within the university.

According to Brown et al. (2001b:27), overall presidents and focus groups agree:

- Diversity and a supportive climate must be presidential priorities; presidents must be willing to hold key administrators accountable for the workplace climate.
- Climate is critical to the successful recruitment and retention of faculty of color.
- Efforts may be formal or informal; a combination of both types works best.
- A diverse climate must exist for all members of the campus com-munity: students, faculty, and staff.
- Dialogue and communication are important; people must feel free to speak about their concerns, and they must know they will be listened to and addressed.
- Sustainability requires the institutionalization of measures that improve the campus climate.
- Policies must be supported by practice.

SUMMARY OF CHALLENGES

This section describes briefly the challenges to recruiting and retaining women undergraduate, graduate, and postdoctoral students and to recruiting and advancing faculty.

Recruiting Women Undergraduates

- Female students are less likely to take higher levels of mathematics prior to enrolling in college and are more likely to concentrate on the biological sciences or chemistry.
- Female students have a less positive view toward successful study of science and mathematics.

Recruiting Women Graduate Students

- Departmental cultures are more of an obstacle for women than for men.
- Universities often lack female-friendly policies.
- Students have negative perceptions of academic careers.

Recruiting Women Postdoctorates

- Postdocs receive insufficient advising and mentoring during the graduate program.
- Postdocs had negative experiences during their graduate careers.
- Postdocs have individual preferences about career goals and views on the relevance of higher education.
- There may be bias against female postdoctoral candidates.

Retaining Women Students

Female undergraduates, graduates, and postdocs face a variety of potential obstacles including

- harassment,
- marginalization and isolation,
- attitudes about career choice,
- lack of role models, and
- curricula perceived as less interesting or less relevant.

Recruiting Women Faculty

- Academe is one of several career choices for both men and women. Women, however, may find major research universities less attractive and be less inclined to seek employment in this sector for the following reasons:
    — Perceptions of working conditions are more negative for women than for men.
    — A lack of diversity in the department and among majors may deter some women from applying.
- Women have less probability of being hired than male candidates for the following reasons:
    — Search committees do not cast a wide net.
    — Search committees submit women to a tougher evaluation than men.

Advancing Women Faculty

- Women faculty have lower rates of tenure and promotion.
- Women faculty must wait longer to receive a promotion.
- Women faculty have lower rates of retention.
- Women faculty have lower job satisfaction.

Finally, there are fewer women top administrators than might be expected by simply viewing the proportion of senior women, because (1) the pipeline may still be small; (2) universities are increasingly searching in areas dominated by male candidates; (3) women are less interested in top administration positions that are viewed as less attractive for women; and (4) discrimination hinders women

SUMMARY OF STRATEGIES

This section describes briefly the strategies useful to educational institutions for recruiting and retaining women undergraduate, graduate, and postdoctoral students and recruiting and advancing faculty.

Recruiting Women Students

- Signal the importance of women.
- Enhance science, engineering, and mathematics education at the K-12 level and at the undergraduate level.
    - Reach out to students at the K-12 level.
- Develop better methods for identifying prospective students.
- Create alternative assessment methods for admissions.

- Organize on-campus orientations.
- Develop bridging programs.
- Extend financial aid.

Retaining Women Students

- Signal the importance of women.
- Improve preparation by enhancing science, engineering, and mathematics education at the K-12 level or through bridging programs and at the undergraduate level.
- Improve advising.
- Establish mentoring programs.
- Change pedagogical approach.
- Increase engagement with students.
- Increase professional socialization.

Recruiting Women Faculty

- Signal the importance of female faculty by means of positive declarative statements, establishing a committee on women, exercising oversight over the hiring process, and devoting resources to hiring women.
- Modify and expand faculty recruiting programs by creating special faculty lines, diversifying search committees, encouraging intervention by deans, and assessing past hiring efforts.
- Improve institutional policies and practices such as the tenure clock, child care, leave, spousal hiring, and training to combat harassment.
- Improve the probability of selection of their graduates as candidates by means of career advising, networking, and enhancing qualifications.

Retaining and Advancing Women Faculty

- Signal the importance of women.
- Create and reinforce female-friendly policies.
- Strengthen mentoring.
- Increase engagement with faculty.

Advancing Women into Leadership Positions

- Conduct an institutional audit.
- Mentor "presidents-in-training."
- Develop executive leadership training opportunities.

- Engage in networking activities.
- Improve the search process.

WHO CAN DO WHAT

Faculty

Valian (1998) identifies several basic strategies that women can utilize to equalize the accumulation of advantage, including working where women are well represented; being impersonal, friendly, and respectful; building power; seeking information; becoming an expert; negotiating, bargaining, and seeking advancement; and overcoming internal barriers to effectiveness. Specific strategies identified in this guide for universities seeking to recruit and retain female students and faculty include

- Network with faculty at community colleges and other four-year institutions to broaden the search for prospective recruits.
- Advise and mentor prospective and current female undergraduate, graduate, and postdoctoral students.
- Conduct outreach to K-12 institutions to help prepare women for college and to combat negative attitudes about the place of women in science and engineering.
- Advise and encourage female students in science and engineering groups.
- Invite female students to participate in research opportunities.
- Participate in bridge programs, campus visits, lectures, and seminars.
- Encourage female students to give presentations at conferences.
- Make curricula more practically relevant and ask whether all students are equally aided by different instructional techniques and technologies.
- Offer career advice and mentoring to doctoral and postdoctoral students.
- Help doctoral and postdoctoral students to compile an application package.
- Treat female faculty respectfully as equal colleagues.
- Be wary of unintentional thinking based on gender schemas.
- Encourage female faculty to aspire to leadership positions and to take advantage of opportunities, both on and off campus, to gain leadership experience.
- Encourage female faculty to network with other female faculty interested in leadership positions and with male and female academic officers.

Department Chairs

• Create an image of the department as female friendly and feature that image in promotional materials and the department's web site.
• Communicate with faculty about the importance of diversity in all areas, including recruiting.
• Support and reinforce a faculty member's commitment to advising and encouraging female students through service awards and recognition during tenure and promotion reviews.
• Monitor the allocation of resources to students and survey students' opinions.
• Broaden admission criteria and cast a wider net in recruiting graduate students.
• Meet with faculty to assess the relationships of curricular content and instruction methods with student learning outcomes for male and female students.
• Make departmental policies and practices transparent.
• Encourage faculty to work with doctoral and postdoctoral students for career placement and support their efforts.
• Diversify search committees.
• Evaluate and broaden efforts to publicize position openings.
• Identify ways to limit service requirements for junior faculty.
• Where possible, modify existing departmental policies and practices—for example, selecting times for standing meetings—so that no type of faculty member is disproportionately affected.
• Make departmental policies and practices transparent.
• Assess the distribution of institutional resources such as lab space and research assistants for fairness.
• Put women on important departmental committees and recommend female faculty for important school-wide or university-wide committees.
• Developing mentoring programs for all faculty.
• Identify ways to limit service requirements for junior faculty.
• Encourage female faculty to gain experience and skills in administration.
• Mentor female faculty on matters of administration.
• Encourage female department chairs to create and use support networks.

Deans and Provosts

• Communicate with department chairs about the importance of diversity in all areas, including recruiting.

- Sponsor competitions, contests, career days, bridge programs, campus orientations, and other efforts to bring prospective students to campus.
- Monitor departments' progress in increasing the percentage of female students and faculty.
- Devote resources to female undergraduate students—support mentoring, advising, tutoring services, and if feasible, separate housing.
- Craft female-friendly policies on campus.
- Communicate with department chairs about the importance of diversity in recruiting.
- Review policies on tenure clock, child care, leave, and spousal hiring. Make policies more transparent.
- Conduct an assessment of departments' progress in increasing the percentage of female students, of recent hiring efforts and outcomes, of trends in the diversity of departments, and of trends in the diversity of administrative appointments.
- Get involved in departmental searches.
- Reinforce human resources programs on sexual and racial discrimination.
- Evaluate recent departmental job offers for fairness in allocation of resources and salary.
- Consider the feasibility of special hiring slots for female faculty.
- Offer incentives to departments that are more inclusive.
- Conduct an assessment of diversity within departments.
- Encourage female faculty to consider leadership positions.
- Develop on-campus leadership programs for faculty.
- Mentor prospective academic officers.
- Encourage female deans and provosts to create and use support networks.

Presidents

- Publicly state the institution's commitment to diversity and inclusiveness whenever possible.
- Create an institutional structure, such as a standing committee, to address diversity issues among the student body, faculty, staff, and administrators. That committee could be charged with monitoring diversity across the institution and with making recommendations to increase diversity.
- Demonstrate the institution's commitment by meeting with students and devoting resources to programs that assist female students.
- Demonstrate the institution's commitment by meeting with faculty, encouraging the use of resources to enhancing hiring strategies, and

examining the institution's policies and practices regarding faculty issues.

- Demonstrate the institution's commitment by meeting with faculty and devoting resources to programs that assist female students and faculty.
- Mentor prospective candidates for executive positions. Mentoring can be done at the same institution or across institutions.
- Conduct a self-assessment of the institution.
- Encourage prospective candidates to enroll in leadership training programs.
- Develop a leadership program on campus.
- Diversify search committees for departmental chair or dean positions.

References

Adelman, C. 1998. Women and Men of the Engineering Path: A Model for Analysis of Undergraduate Careers. Office of Educational Research and Improvement, U.S. Department of Education. Washington, D.C.: Government Printing Office.

Amenkhienan, C. A., and L. R. Kogan. 2004. Engineering students' perceptions of academic activities and support services: Factors that influence their academic performance. College Student Journal 38:4.

Andruskiw, O., and N. J. Howes. 1980. Dispelling a myth: That stereotypic attitudes influence evaluations of women as administrators in higher education. Journal of Higher Education 51(5):475–496.

Anonymous. 1998. A ten-point checklist for assessing presidential commitment to diversity. Black Issues in Higher Education 15(20):30.

Anonymous. 2003. University of Nebraska increases women, minority hiring, but still falls short of goal. Black Issues in Higher Education 19(25):9.

Anonymous. 2005. Princeton, Smith College partner to increase women in engineering. Black Issues in Higher Education 21(25):12.

Ash, A. S., P. L. Carr, R. Goldstein, and R. H. Friedman. 2004. Compensation and advancement of women in academic medicine: Is there equity? Annals of Internal Medicine 141(3):205–212.

Astin, H. S., and C. M. Cress. 2003. A national profile of academic women in research universities. Pp. 53–88 in Equal Rites, Unequal Outcomes: Women in American Research Universities. L. S. Hornig, ed. New York: Kluwer Academic/Plenum Publishers.

August, L., and J. Waltman. 2004. Culture, climate, and contribution: Career satisfaction among female faculty. Research in Higher Education 45(2):177–192.

Babcock, L., and S. Laschever. 2003. Women Don't Ask: Negotiation and the Gender Divide. Princeton, N.J.: Princeton University Press.

Basinger, J. 2001. Struggling for a balanced life as a president. Chronicle of Higher Education, April 27.

Basinger, J. 2002. Casting a wider net. Chronicle of Higher Education, December 13.

118

Berkner, L., S. He, and E. F. Cataldi. 2002. Descriptive Summary of 1995–96 Beginning Postsecondary Students: Six Years Later (NCES 2003–151). National Center for Education Statistics, U.S. Department of Education. Washington, D.C.: Government Printing Office.

Bhattacharjee, Y. 2004. Family matters: Stopping tenure clock may not be enough. Science 306(5704):2031, 2033.

Black, H. 1999. Living and studying together. The Scientist 13(23):6.

Blum, D. E. 1990. 165 female college presidents 'honor progress, connect with each other,' and commiserate. Chronicle of Higher Education, December 19.

Blum, L. 2001. Transforming the culture of computing at Carnegie Mellon. Available at http://www-2.cs.cmu.edu/~lblum/PAPERS/TransformingTheCulture.pdf. Accessed April 6, 2005.

Boyle, P., and B. Boice. 1998. Best practices for enculturation: Collegiality, mentoring, and structure. New Directions in Higher Education 101(spring):87–94.

Bozeman, S. T., and R. J. Hughes. 2004. Improving the graduate school experience for women in mathematics: The EDGE Program. Journal of Women and Minorities in Science and Engineering 10:243–253.

Brainard, J. 2005. Postdoctoral researchers value structured training over pay, survey says. Chronicle of Higher Education, April 15.

Brown, G., C. Van Ummersen, and J. Sturnick. 2001a. Breaking the Barriers: Presidential Strategies for Enhancing Career Mobility. Washington, D.C.: American Council on Education.

Brown, G., C. Van Ummersen, and J. Sturnick. 2001b. From Where We Sit: Women's Perspectives on the Presidency. Washington, D.C.: American Council on Education.

Brown, G., C. Van Ummersen, and J. Sturnick. 2002. Breaking the Barriers: A Guidebook of Strategies. Washington, D.C.: American Council on Education.

Busch-Vishniac, I., and J. Jarosz. 2004. Can diversity in the undergraduate engineering population be enhanced through curricular change. Journal of Women and Minorities in Science and Engineering 10:255–281.

Carr, P. L., A. S. Ash, R. H. Friedman, L. Szalacha, R. C. Barnett, A. Palepu, and M. M. Moskowitz. 2000. Faculty perceptions of gender discrimination and sexual harassment in academic medicine. Annals of Internal Medicine 132(11):889–896.

Chacon, P., and H. Soto-Johnson. 2003. Encouraging young women to stay in the mathematics pipeline: Mathematics camps for young women. School Science and Mathematics 103(6):274–284.

College Board. 2005. Advanced Placement Report to the Nation. New York: College Board.

Committee on Graduate Education, Association of American Universities (AAU). 1998. Report and Recommendations. Washington, D.C.: AAU. Available at http://www.aau.edu/reports/GradEdRpt.html. Accessed April 7, 2005.

COSEPUP (Committee on Science, Engineering, and Public Policy). 1997. Adviser, Teacher, Role Model, Friend: On Being a Mentor to Students in Science and Engineering. Washington, D.C.: National Academy Press.

COSEPUP. 2000. Enhancing the Postdoctoral Experience for Scientists and Engineers: A Guide for Postdoctoral Scholars, Advisers, Institutions, Funding Organizations, and Disciplinary Societies. Washington, D.C.: National Academy Press.

Cuny, J., and W. Aspray. 2001. Recruitment and Retention of Women Graduate Students in Computer Science and Engineering. Washington, D.C.: Computing Research Association.

Davis, G. 2005. Doctors without orders: Highlights of the Sigma Xi postdoc survey. American Scientist (Special Supplement) 93(3):1–13. Available at http://postdoc.sigmaxi.org/results/. Accessed March 3, 2006.

Denecke, D. D. 2004. Ph.D. completion headlines. CGS Communicator 37(1):1, 4, 7.

Dowdall, J. 2004. The right search committee. Chronicle of Higher Education, July 30.

Etzkowitz, H., C. Kemelgor, M. Neuschatz, B. Uzzi, and J. Alonzo. 1994. The paradox of critical mass for women in science. Science 266(5182):51–54.

Farrell, E. F. 2002. Engineering a warmer welcome for female students. Chronicle of Higher Education, February 22.

Ferreira, M. M. 2003. Gender issues related to graduate student attrition in two science departments. International Journal of Science Education 25(8):969–989.

Ferrer de Valero, Y. 2001. Departmental factors affecting time-to-degree and completion rates of doctoral students at one land-grant research institution. Journal of Higher Education 72(3):341–367.

Fisher, A., and J. Margolis. 2002. Unlocking the Clubhouse: Women in Computing. Cambridge, Mass.: MIT Press.

Fogg, P. 2003a. So many committees, so little time. Chronicle of Higher Education 50(17):A14.

Fogg, P. 2003b. The gap that won't go away: Women continue to lag behind men in pay; the reasons may have little to do with gender bias. Chronicle of Higher Education, April 18.

Fogg, P. 2004. U. of Colorado fires longtime professor for sexually harassing students. Chronicle of Higher Education, April 30.

Fox, M. F. 2001. Women, science, and academia: Graduate education and careers. Gender and Society 15(5):654–666.

Freeman, C. E. 2004. Trends in educational equity of girls and women: 2004. NCES 2005-016. National Center for Education Statistics, U.S. Department of Education. Washington, D.C.: Government Printing Office.

Fried, L. P., C. A. Francomano, S. M. MacDonald, E. M. Wagner, E. J. Stokes, K. M. Carbone, W. B. Bias, M. M. Newman, and J. D. Stobo. 1996. Career development for women in academic medicine: Multiple interventions in a department of medicine. JAMA 276(11): 898–905.

Fry, C., and S. Allgood. 2002. The effect of female student participation in the Society of Women Engineers on retention: A study at Baylor University. Paper presented at the 32nd ASEE/IEEE Frontiers in Education Conference, FRC-15, Boston, November 6–9, 2002.

Gibbons, M. 2003. Engineering on the rise. In 2002 Profiles of Engineering and Engineering Technology Colleges. Washington, D.C.: American Society for Engineering Education.

Gibbons, M. 2004. A new look at engineering. Statistics from 2003 edition of the Profiles of Engineering and Engineering Technology Colleges. Available at http://www.asee. org/about/publications/profiles/upload/2003engprofile.pdf. Accessed August 2, 2004.

Ginther, D. 2001. Does science discriminate against women? Evidence from academia, 1973–97. Federal Reserve Bank of Atlanta Working Paper 2001-02.

Ginther, D. 2004. Why women earn less: Economic explanations for the gender salary gap in science. AWIS Magazine 33(1):6–10.

Ginther, D., and S. Kahn. 2006. Does Science Promote Women? Evidence from Academia 1973-2001. Unpublished manuscript, February 17.

Golde, C. M. 1998. Beginning graduate school: Explaining first-year doctoral attrition. New Directions for Higher Education 101:55–64.

Golde, C. M. 2000. Should I stay or should I go? Student descriptions of the doctoral attrition process. Review of Higher Education 23(2):199–227.

Gonzalez, C. 2001. Undergraduate Research, Graduate Mentoring, and the University's Mission. Science 293(5535):1624–1626.

Haro, R. P. 1991. Women continue to be ignored for presidencies (letter to the editor). New York Times, December 4.

Holmen, B. A., and L. Aultman-Hall. 2005. Women in Engineering Leadership Summit: Conference Overview and Summary. May 3–5, 2004, Storrs, Conn. Available at http://www.weli.eng.iastate.edu/Documents/Leadership%20Summit_Conn/Summit%20White%20Paper%20Publication_w_Covers.pdf. Accessed April 20, 2005.

Ivie, R. 2004. Women physics and astronomy faculty. Presentation at meeting of Committee on Gender Differences in Careers of Science, Engineering, and Mathematics Faculty, National Academies, Washington, D.C., January 29, 2004.

Kerber, L. K. 2005. We must make the academic workplace more humane and equitable. Chronicle of Higher Education, March 18.

Kinkead, J. 2003. Learning through inquiry: An overview of undergraduate research. New Directions for Teaching and Learning 93:5–18.

Kirkman, E., J. Maxwell, and K. R. Priestley. 2003. 2002 annual survey of the mathematical sciences (third report). Notices of the AMS, September 2003, 925–935.

Knight, M. T., and C. M. Cunningham. 2004. Building a structure of support: An inside look at the structure of women in engineering programs. Journal of Women and Minorities in Science and Engineering 10:1–20.

Kreeger, K. 2004. Healthy limits. Nature (January 8):178–179.

Kulis, S., and D. Sicotte. 2002. Women scientists in academia: Geographically constrained to big cities, college clusters, or the coasts? Research in Higher Education 43(1):1–30.

Lancy, D. F. 2003. What one faculty member does to promote undergraduate research. New Directions for Teaching and Learning 93:87–92.

Landrum, R. E., and M. A. Clump. 2004. Departmental search committees and the evaluation of faculty applicants. Teaching of Psychology 31(1):12–17.

Lau, L. K. 2003. Institutional factors affecting student retention. Education 124(1):126–136.

Lawler, A. 1999. Tenured women battle to make it less lonely at the top. Science 286:1272–1278.

Lively, K. 2000a. Female provosts weight many factors in deciding whether to seek presidencies. Chronicle of Higher Education, June 16.

Lively, K. 2000b. Women in charge. Chronicle of Higher Education, June 16.

Long, J. S., P. Allison, and R. McGinnis. 1993. Rank advancement in academic careers: Sex differences and the effects of productivity. American Sociological Review 58(5): 703–722.

Lopatto, D. 2005. The benefits of undergraduate research. Academic Leader 21(2):3.

Lovitts, B. E. 2001. Leaving the Ivory Tower: The Causes and Consequences of Departure from Doctoral Study. Lanham, Md.: Rowman and Littlefield.

Marra, R. M., and B. Bogue. 2004. The Assessing Women in Engineering Project: A model for sustainable and profitable collaboration. Journal of Women and Minorities in Science and Engineering 10:283–295.

Mason, M. A., and M. Goulden. 2002. Do babies matter? Academe 88(6):21–28.

MIT (Massachusetts Institute of Technology). 1999. A study on the status of women faculty in science at MIT: How a Committee on Women Faculty came to be established by the dean of the School of Science, what the committee and the dean learned and accomplished, and recommendations for the future. MIT Faculty Newsletter 11(March).

McGinn, D. 2005. Gender: Formula for success. Newsweek, March 14.

McNeil, L., and M. Sher. 1999. The dual-career-couple problem. Physics Today 52(7):32–37.

Merkel, C. A. 2003. Undergraduate research at the research universities. New Directions for Teaching and Learning 93:39–53.

Moody, J. 2004. Supporting women and minority faculty. Academe 90(1):47–52.

NAE (National Academy of Engineering) and NRC (National Research Council). 2005. Enhancing the Community College Pathway to Engineering Careers. M. Mattis and J. Sislin, eds. Washington, D.C.: National Academy Press.

NRC (National Research Council). 1996. The Path to the Ph.D.: Measuring Graduate Attrition in the Sciences and Humanities. Washington, D.C.: National Academy Press.

NRC. 2001. From Scarcity to Visibility: Gender Differences in the Careers of Doctoral Scientists and Engineers. J. S. Long, ed. Washington, D.C.: National Academy Press.

NSB (National Science Board). 2004. Science and Engineering Indicators 2004. 2 vols. Arlington, Va.: National Science Foundation (vol. 1, NSB 04-1; vol. 2, NSB 04-1A).

NSF (National Science Foundation). 1997. Women and Science: Celebrating Achievements, Charting Challenges. Arlington, Va.

NSF. 1999. Women, Minorities, and Persons with Disabilities in Science and Engineering: 1998. NSF 99-338. Arlington, Va.

NSF. 2001. Women, Minorities, and Persons with Disabilities in Science and Engineering: 2000. NSF 00-327. Arlington, Va.

NSF, Division of Science Resources Statistics. 2003. Characteristics of Doctoral Scientists and Engineers in the United States: 2001. NSF 03-310. Project Officer, K. H. Kang. Arlington, Va.

NSF, Division of Science Resources Statistics. 2004a. Gender Differences in the Careers of Academic Scientists and Engineers. NSF 04-323. Project Officer, A. I. Rapoport. Arlington, Va.

NSF, Division of Science Resources Statistics. 2004b. Science and Engineering Degrees: 1966–2001. NSF 04-311. Project Officers, S. T. Hill and J. M. Johnson. Arlington, Va.

NSF, Division of Science Resources Statistics. 2004c. Women, Minorities, and Persons with Disabilities in Science and Engineering: 2004. NSF 04-317. Arlington, Va. (updated May 2004).

NSF, Division of Science Resources Statistics. 2005. Graduate Students and Postdoctorates in Science and Engineering: Fall 2002. NSF 05-310. Project Officers, J. D. Oliver and E. B. Rivers. Arlington, Va.

Nelson, D. J., and D. C. Rogers. 2004. A national analysis of diversity in science and engineering faculties at research universities. Unpublished. University of Oklahoma.

Nicklin, J. L. 2001. Few women are among the presidents with the largest compensation packages. Chronicle of Higher Education, November 9.

Packard, B. W.-L. 2003. Web-based mentoring: Challenging traditional models to increase women's access. Mentoring and Tutoring 11(1):53–65.

Park, S. 1996. Research, teaching, and service: Why shouldn't women's work count? Journal of Higher Education 67(1):46–84.

Perna, L. 2002. Sex differences in the supplemental earnings of college and university faculty. Research in Higher Education 43(1):31–58.

Perna, L. 2003. Studying faculty salary equity: A review of theoretical and methodological approaches. In Higher Education: Handbook of Theory and Research, Vol. 18, J. C. Smart, ed. New York: Kluwer Academic Publishers.

Persell, C. H. 1983. Gender, rewards and research in education. Psychology of Women Quarterly 8(1):33–47.

Peter, K., and L. Horn. 2005. Gender Differences in Participation and Completion of Undergraduate Education and How They Have Changed Over Time. NCES 2005–169. National Center for Education Statistics, U.S. Department of Education. Washington, D.C.: Government Printing Office.

Quinn, K., S. E. Lange, and S. G. Olswang. 2004. Family-friendly policies and the research university. Academe 90(6):32–34.

Raines, S. C., and M. S. Alberg. 2003. The role of professional development in preparing academic leaders. New Directions for Higher Education 124(winter):33–39.

Rankin, S., III. 2004. Studying gender differences among science, engineering, and mathematics faculty. Presentation at meeting of Committee on Gender Differences in Careers of Science, Engineering, and Mathematics Faculty, National Academies, Washington, D.C., January 29, 2004.

Rankin, P., and J. Nielsen. 2004. NETWORKING—Why you need to know people who know people. Available at http://advance.colorado.edu/research_networking1/. Accessed April 20, 2005.

Rivard, N. 2003. Who's running the show? University Business 6(2):11–13.

Rosser, S. V., and J. Z. Daniels. 2004. Widening paths to success, improving the environment, and moving toward lessons learned from the experiences of POWRE and CBL awardees. Journal of Women and Minorities in Science and Engineering 10(2):131–148.

Santovec, M. L. 2004. Priming the pump: CAOs move to the college presidency. Women in Higher Education, June. Available at http://www.wihe.com. Accessed April 20, 2005.

Schackner, B. 2005. Diversity rules among state system's university presidents. Pittsburgh Post-Gazette, February 4.

Schneider, A. 2000. Female scientists turn their backs on jobs at research universities. Chronicle of Higher Education, August 18.

Schroeder, K. 1998. Science majors defect. Education Digest 63(6):75–76.

Seymour, E., and N. M. Hewitt. 1997. Talking about Leaving: Why Undergraduates Leave the Sciences. Boulder, Colo.: Westview Press.

Siegel, L. 2005. A study of Ph.D. completion at Duke University. CGS Communicator 38(1): 1–2, 6–7.

Steinpreis, R. E., K. A. Anders, and D. Ritzke. 1999. The impact of gender on the review of the curricula vitae of job applicants and tenure candidates: A national empirical study. Sex Roles 41(7/8):509–528.

Sullivan, B., C. Hollenshead, and G. Smith. 2004. Developing and implementing work-family policies for faculty. Academe 90(6):24–27.

Symonds, W. 2004. A breakthrough for MIT—and science. BusinessWeek, October 4, 98–100.

Tesch, B. J., H. M. Wood, A. L. Helwig, and A. B. Nattinger. 1995. Promotion of women physicians in academic medicine: Glass ceiling or sticky floor? JAMA 273(13):1022–1025.

Trower, C., and R. Chait. 2002. Faculty diversity. Harvard Magazine, March–April, 33–37, 98.

University of Pennsylvania. 2003. Gender equity: Penn's second annual report. Available at http://www.upenn.edu/almanac/v50/n16/gender_equity.html. Accessed April 28, 2005.

University of Wisconsin ADVANCE Program. 2005. Faculty hiring: Diversity and excellence go hand-in-hand, updated February 28, 2005. Available at http://www.engr. washington.edu/advance/resources/Diversity-and-Excellence.pdf. Accessed April 20, 2005.

US DOE (U.S. Department of Education). 2001. Exemplary and Promising Gender Equity Programs 2000. Washington, D.C.: U.S. Department of Education.

US DOE, National Center for Education Statistics. 2000. Entry and Persistence of Women and Minorities in College Science and Engineering Education. NCES 2000-601. Washington, D.C.: Government Printing Office.

US DOE, National Center for Education Statistics. 2004. The Condition of Education 2004. NCES 2004-077. Washington, D.C.: Government Printing Office.

Valian, V. 1998. Why So Slow? The Advancement of Women. Cambridge, Mass.: MIT Press.

Valian, V. 2004. Beyond gender schemas: Improving the advancement of women in academia. NWSA Journal 16(1):207–220.

Van Ummersen, C. 2001. Finally, big women on campus (letter to the editor). New York Times, September 10, 28.

Ward, K., and L. Wolf-Wendel. 2004. Fear factor: How safe is it to make time for family? Academe 90(6):28–31.

Whitten, B. L., et al. 2003. What works? Increasing the participation of women in undergraduate physics. Journal of Women and Minorities in Science and Engineering 9: 239–258.

Wilson, R. 2003. Duke and Princeton will spend more to make female professors happy. Chronicle of Higher Education, October 10.

Wilson, R. 2004a. Students sue professor and U. of Texas in harassment case. Chronicle of Higher Education, July 2.

Wilson, R. 2004b. Where the elite teach, it's still a man's world. Chronicle of Higher Education, December 3.

Wolf-Wendel, L., S. B. Twombly, and S. Rice. 2003. The Two-Body Problem: Dual-Career-Couple Hiring Practices in Higher Education. Baltimore, Md.: The Johns Hopkins University Press.

Xie, Y., and K. Shauman. 2003. Women in Science. Cambridge, Mass: Harvard University Press.

Zernike. K. 2001. Playing in the big league. New York Times, September 9, 82.

Index

A

AASCU. *See* American Association of State Colleges and Universities
AAUP. *See* American Association of University Professors
ACE. *See* American Council on Education
ACE Fellows Program, 105
ACE Network, 106
Action steps, 114–117
  for deans and provosts, 47, 70, 85, 99, 108, 115–116
  for department chairs, 47, 70, 85, 99, 108, 115
  for faculty, 47, 70, 85, 99, 108, 114
  for presidents, 47, 70, 85, 99, 108, 116–117
Administrative positions, policies to advance women into, 3
Admissions process, revising, 36
Advanced placement (AP) examinees, 15–17
  in computer science, 33
Advice networks, 59. *See also* Student advising
Adviser, Teacher, Role Model, Friend: On Being a Mentor to Students in Science and Engineering, 60
African American female students, 18–23, 37

Alienation within departments, a cultural barrier facing women faculty, 91–93
American Association of State Colleges and Universities (AASCU), 104–106
American Association of University Professors (AAUP), 6
American College President Study, 101
American Council on Education (ACE), 101, 106–107
AP. *See* Advanced placement examinees
Asian American female students, 18–23, 37
ASPIRE (Alabama Supercomputing Program to Inspire Computational Research in Education) project, 33
Assessments, collecting statistics needed for, 82
Association of American Universities, 66
Audits. *See* Institutional audits

B

Bachelor's degrees awarded
  by field and gender, 17–18
  in science and engineering, number of women receiving, 28
Baylor University, 63
Benefits
  access to medical and dental, 45–46
  lower for women faculty, 102

Big sister/little sister programs, 59
Black female students, 18–23, 37
Bridging programs, developing, 39
Bring Your Daughter to Work Day, 36
Bryn Mawr College, 105

C

Candidates
    casting a broader net to identify,
        81–82
    improving the positions of, 83–84
Career Day for Girls, 36
Carnegie Corporation, 106
Carnegie Mellon University, 56
Celebration of women in computing, 59
Center for Policy Analysis, 107
Challenges, faced by female students and
        faculty, 5–8, 30, 55, 77, 93, 103, 111–
        112
Chicana students, 18–23
Child care policies
    establishing, 45, 82–83
    reinforcing, 95
Chronicle of Higher Education, 102
Committee on Graduate Education, 66
Committee on Science, Engineering, and
        Public Policy (COSEPUP), 11, 68
Committee on the Guide to Recruiting and
        Advancing Women Scientists and
        Engineers in Academia, 1
Committee on the Status of Women in
        Computing Research, 42
Committee on Women in Science and
        Engineering (CWSE), 1, 8–9, 100
Computer science and engineering (CSE)
    celebration of women in, 59
    majors in, 42
Computing Research Association, 42
Constructive feedback, providing, 68
COSEPUP. See Committee on Science,
        Engineering, and Public Policy
CSE. See Computer science and
        engineering

D

Day-to-day policies, changing, 96
Deans and provosts, action steps for, 47,
        70, 85, 99, 108, 115–116

Departmental issues
    action steps for chairs, 47, 70, 85, 99,
        108, 115
    cultural alienation women faculty face,
        53–54, 91–93
    funding, 54
Diversity. See also Inclusiveness
    advisory councils for, 32
    setting targets for, 32
Doctoral degrees awarded
    by broad field and gender, 72
    in science and engineering, number of
        women receiving, 28
DOE. See U.S. Department of Education
Duke University, 48
Duties, allowing modification of, 96

E

Enhancing the Postdoctoral Experience for
        Scientists and Engineers: A Guide for
        Postdoctoral Scholars, Advisers,
        Institutions, Funding Organizations,
        and Disciplinary Societies, 30
EQUALS, 33–34
Equity of salaries and resources, instituting
        regular studies to determine, 45
Executive leadership training, to help
        women advance to executive
        positions, 105–106
Executive positions, recruiting and
        advancing women to, 108

F

Faculty members, action steps for, 47, 70,
        85, 99, 108, 114
Faculty recruitment programs
    casting a broader net to identify
        candidates, 81–82
    collecting statistics on hiring processes
        and outcomes to aid in assessments,
        82
    engaging in focused faculty recruiting, 81
    having institutional executives
        intervene, 82
    modifying or expanding, 81–82
    policies to enhance, 3
    providing incentive grants, 81
    taking steps to diversify search
        committees, 81

Family-friendly policies, 27, 45–46
Feedback, providing constructive, 68
Freshmen intending to major in S&E, by race/ethnicity, gender, and field, 20–24
Funding for graduate students. *See also* Research assistantships
providing secure, 67–68

G

Gender disparities, in U.S. academia, 5–8
Gender inclusiveness, 2
Graduate S&E programs, enhancing and improving, 44–45
Graduate S&E students, 39–43, 47, 70
challenges of recruiting women, 25–29, 111
challenges of retaining women, 53–54
enhancing and improving undergraduate S&E programs, 42
identifying prospective students, 42
offering financial aid, 43
organizing on-campus orientations, 42–43
signaling the importance of women, 40–41
strategies for recruiting women, 39
strategies for retaining women, 65
women underrepresented among, 1
Grants, providing incentive, 81

H

Harassment by gender, perception and experience of, 52, 89
Henry Luce Foundation, The, 88
High school graduates, percentage taking mathematics and science in high school, by gender, 16
Hiring processes and outcomes, collecting statistics to aid in assessments, 82
Housing subsidies, offering, 45–46

I

Incentive grants, providing, 81
Inclusiveness, 2
"Inspired" individuals, 77

Institutional audits, to help women advance to executive positions, 104
Institutional executives, intervention by, 82
Institutional policies and practices
creating spousal hiring programs, 83
establishing parental leave policies and child care, 82–83
extending the tenure clock, 82
improving to recruit women faculty, 82–83
instituting sexual harassment sensitivity programs, 83
Institutional resources, fewer available to women faculty, 90–91

J

Job satisfaction, among women faculty, 88
Johns Hopkins University, 88
Junior faculty, limiting service among, 95–96

L

Leadership positions. *See also* Executive leadership training
strategies for advancing women into, 113–114
Low-income parents, 95

M

Massachusetts Institute of Technology (MIT), 90–91
Master's degrees awarded, in science and engineering, number of women receiving, 28
Medical and dental benefits, offering access to, 45–46
Mentoring programs
establishing, 58–60
to help "presidents-in-training," 104–105
to help women faculty, 96–98
improving, 66–67
Methodology issues, 9–11
Mexican American female students, 18–23
Millennium Leadership Initiative (MLI), 105

MIT. *See* Massachusetts Institute of Technology
MLI. *See* Millennium Leadership Initiative
Modified duties, allowing for, 96

N

National Academies, 1, 9, 11, 60, 66
National Center for Education Statistics, 49
National Council of Chief Academic Officers, 104
National Institutes of Health (NIH), 46
National Research Council, 30
National Research Service Awards (NRSA), 46
National Science Foundation (NSF), 6, 27, 33–35, 87
National Survey of Postsecondary Faculty (NSOPF), 89n
National Survey of Recent College Graduates, 35n
Networking. *See also* Advice networks
to help women advance to executive positions, 106
NIH. *See* National Institutes of Health
NRSA. *See* National Research Service Awards
NSF. *See* National Science Foundation
NSOPF. *See* National Survey of Postsecondary Faculty

O

Office of Women in Higher Education (OWHE), 106
On-campus orientations, organizing, 36–38, 42–43
Orientations, organizing on-campus, 36–38, 42–43
OWHE. *See* Office of Women in Higher Education

P

Parental leave policies
establishing, 45, 82–83
reinforcing, 95
Pedagogical changes needed, 60–61

Policies and practices that advance women faculty, 3
allowing modified duties, 96
changing day-to-day policies, 96
equity of salaries and resources, 45
female- and family-friendly policies, 45–46
limiting service among junior faculty, 95–96
offering housing subsidies and access to medical and dental benefits, 45–46
parental leave policies and child care, 45, 82–83, 95
periodic reviews and adjustments of salaries, 96
sexual harassment sensitivity programs, 45, 95
Postdoctoral S&E students
challenges of recruiting women, 29–30, 111
enhancing and improving the graduate experience, 44–45
establishing female- and family-friendly policies and practices, 45–46
by gender, 29
identifying prospective students, 45
increasing salaries of, 46
signaling the importance of women, 44
strategies for recruiting women, 43–47
strategies for retaining women, 70
women underrepresented among, 1
Presidents, action steps for, 47, 70, 85, 99, 108, 116–117
"Presidents-in-training," 104–105
Princeton University, 38, 103
Professional socialization, increasing, 63–65, 67
Program for Gender Equity, 34n
Promotion rates, women faculty facing lower, 87
Prospective students, identifying, 42, 45
Provosts. *See* Deans and provosts
Puerto Rican American female students, 18–23

R

Recruiting women faculty, 1, 71–85
challenges of, 72–77
strategies for, 78–84

Recruiting women students, 14–47
    challenges of, 14–30
    strategies for, 30–47
Research assistantships, 43
Research questions, 8–9
Research time, of women faculty,
        inadequate protection of, 89–90
Resources, determining equity of access to,
        45
Retaining women graduate students, 65–68
    improving mentoring, 66–67
    increasing professional socialization, 67
    providing constructive feedback, 68
    providing secure funding for graduate
        students, 67–68
    signaling the importance of women, 65–
        66
Retaining women postdoctoral fellows, 68–
        69
Retaining women students, 3, 48–70
    challenges of, 49–55
    strategies for, 55–69
Retaining women undergraduate students,
        55–65
    establishing mentoring programs, 58–60
    increasing engagement with women
        students, 61–63
    increasing professional socialization,
        63–65
    making pedagogical changes, 60–61
    signaling the importance of women, 56–
        57
    strengthening student advising, 57–58
Retention rates, women faculty facing
        lower, 88
Rutgers, the State University of New
        Jersey, 62

S

Salaries
    instituting regular studies to determine
        equity of, 45, 110
    undertaking periodic reviews and
        adjustments of, 96
Science, 44
Science and engineering (S&E) enterprise,
        1–3
    doctoral degrees awarded to women,
        by field, 74–75

    enhancing education and outreach
        efforts at the K-12 level, 33–35
    female graduate students, by field, 26
    national "talent" in finding talent for,
        40
    number of women receiving degrees in,
        28
    preparation for, 51–52
    showing interest in high school, 48
Search process
    for applicants, broadening, 35–36
    changing to help women advance to
        executive positions, 107
    diversifying committees for, 81
Service, limiting among junior faculty, 95–
        96
Sexual harassment
    instituting sensitivity programs for, 45,
        83
    reinforcing sensitivity programs for, 95
Smith College, 38
Social events, 36–38, 42–43, 59
Society of Women Engineers (SWE), 36, 63
Spousal hiring programs, creating, 83
Statistics needed for assessments,
        collecting, 82
Strategies for advancing women faculty,
        94–98
    creating and reinforcing policies and
        practices, 95–96
    engaging women faculty more fully in
        the institution, 98
    signaling the importance of women, 94–
        95
    strengthening mentoring, 96–98
Strategies for advancing women to
        executive positions, 103–107
    changing the search process, 107
    conducting an institutional audit, 104
    developing executive leadership
        training, 105–106
    engaging in networking, 106
    mentoring "presidents-in-training,"
        104–105
Strategies for recruiting women faculty,
        78–84
    improving institutional policies and
        practices, 82–83
    improving the positions of candidates,
        83–84

modifying or expanding faculty
   recruitment programs, 81–82
signaling the importance of women
   faculty, 78–80
Strategies for recruiting women students,
   30–47
   graduate student recruitment, 39–43
   policies to enhance, 2–3
   postdoctoral recruiting, 43–46
   undergraduate student recruitment, 30–
      39
Students. See also Graduate S&E students;
   Postdoctoral S&E students;
   Undergraduate S&E students;
   Women students
   strengthening advising of, 57–58
Summer Institute for Women in Higher
   Education Administration, 105

T

Team-oriented courses, 60n
Tenure-track faculty issues, 72
   extending the tenure clock for women,
      82
   males and females tenured at top 50
      U.S. educational institutions, 76
   women faculty facing lower tenure
      rates, 87
Tilghman, Shirley, 38, 103
Time to promotion, women faculty facing
   longer, 87
Training. See Executive leadership
   training

U

Undergraduate S&E programs, enhancing
   and improving, 42
Undergraduate S&E students
   broadening the search for applicants,
      35–36
   celebrating research work of, 64
   challenges of recruiting women, 15–25,
      111
   challenges of retaining women, 49–53
   developing bridging programs, 39
   enhancing S&E education and outreach
      efforts at the K-12 level, 33–35

freshmen intending to major in S&E,
   20–24
organizing on-campus orientations, 36–
   38
residence halls for women in, 62
revising the admissions process, 36
signaling the importance of women, 32–
   33
strategies for recruiting women, 30–39,
   47
strategies for retaining women, 55, 70
University of Pennsylvania, 82
University of Southern California, 64
University of Southern Colorado, 37
U.S. Department of Education (DOE), 15,
   25, 49
U.S. News and World Report, 13

W

White female students, 18–23
Why So Slow, 77
WIE. See Women in Engineering
WISE. See Women in Science and
   Engineering
Women, Minorities, and Persons with
   Disabilities in Science and Engineering,
   6
Women advancing
   in four institutions, 11–13, 109–110
   signaling the importance of, 32–33, 40–
      41, 44, 56–57, 65–66, 94–95
Women advancing to executive positions,
   100–108
   challenges faced by, 101–103
   strategies for, 103–107
Women faculty, challenges faced by, 86–99,
   112
   alienating departmental cultures, 91–93
   fewer institutional resources, 90–91
   isolation, 92–93
   longer time to promotion, 87
   lower benefits, 102
   lower job satisfaction, 88
   lower retention rates, 88
   lower tenure and promotion rates, 87
   marginalization, 92
   research time inadequately protected,
      89–90
   work-family conflicts, 91

Women faculty, strategies for advancing, 1,
    86–99. *See also* Policies and practices
    that advance women faculty
  engaging more fully in the institution,
    54, 98
  recruitment strategies, 85, 113
  retention and advancement strategies,
    94–99, 113
  signaling the importance of women, 78–
    80
Women in Engineering (WIE), 63
Women in Science and Engineering
    (WISE), 63
Women Presidents Network, 104, 106

Women Professionals from Industry, 36
Women students, 3, 14–30, 49–55
  challenges faced by, 111
  increasing engagement with, 61–63
  race and ethnicity of, 18–23
  recruiting graduate students, 25–29
  recruiting postdocs, 29–30
  recruiting undergraduates, 15–25
  retaining graduate students, 53–54
  retaining undergraduates, 49–53
  strategies to advance, 112–113
Work-family conflicts, women faculty
    facing, 91